erniehurwitz @

steve:
hurwitz.steven@yahoo.com

JAN 2024

DIANE,
SHARING MY 15 MINUTES
OF FAME FOR YOUR
FAMILY TREE.
LOVE
Ernie

ACKNOWLEDGEMENTS

The project organization, editing, graphic design, fact-checking, legal confirmation, photo digitizing, book layout, press release, distribution, and so much more was skillfully done by a Hurwitz:
Anna, Martha, Dan, and Lila.
…a loving gesture that I will always cherish.

Janine St. Germaine, who took me to Grand Central Station, many years ago, to tell my story to StoryCorps.

Maha Bendet, for her professional encouragement.

Barbara Burn, who I met in Alaska, who first edited my memoir.

David Prete, who told me to "Go for it!"

The memoir writing class at Lifetime Learning Center in Seattle, who heard each of these stories and steered me into writing "in my own voice."

My wife, Kaveri, who heard these stories endlessly and edited the first and final written versions with love and support.

…and, of course, to Dicky, Niki, and Billy… R.I.P.

THANK YOU   THANK YOU   THANK YOU

CONTENTS

PROLOGUE

Aeroflot jet from Brussels to Moscow, 1959.

The full realization of where I was going came when a firm hand grabbed my wrist and I heard a thickly accented woman saying, "You cannot take pictures when we are flying over Russian territory."

I was in a Russian airliner flying to Russia with four other Americans. Russia and the United States had been in a Cold War since 1945—basically two countries hostile to the verge of open warfare.

I was a 27-year-old construction project manager going to build a house in a park in Moscow, Russia, in the summer of 1959. I grew up during WWII when Russia was our ally. Now they were pointing missiles at the United States and I was going to spend almost a month with my own country's missiles pointing at me.

Despite that anxiety, I looked forward to experiencing some of the things I knew about Russia: eating cabbage and boiled potatoes, visiting Stalin and Lenin at the Kremlin, and meeting *babushka*-wearing Russian women. I had just left New York City where Fifth Avenue models were always in view and even the street food was considered fine cuisine.

What follows are some stories from the trip that radically changed my perception of Russia. But that's not the whole story. I accidentally became part of a globally historic event that may have moved fingers closer to the Red Button.

Aeroflot Brussels to Moscow flight plan.

1 SPLITNIK

Crowds at the American National Exhibition in Moscow, 1959.

"Nixon and Khrushchev are headed in the wrong direction!" Billy shouted. "Take down the fences so they can walk into the right side of the house!"

"Billy" was part of the U.S. team responsible for building a model American house in Moscow in July of 1959, in the middle of the Cold War. He would become famous for his role in helping to stage the historic debate that was held in the kitchen of the model house I built with the help of four New York City-based construction workers.

Billy's real name was William Safire; he later became President Nixon's speech writer and the conservative columnist for *The New York Times*. In the summer of 1959, however, he was a public relations man for the firm that was instrumental in getting my boss's home-building company to participate in a trade fair in Moscow. Government diplomats thought the event might ease tensions between the two nations.

The idea for the trade fair was that the United States would take everyday products from America to Russia, and the Russians would display their products at the Coliseum in New York City. The Russians focused on Sputnik, the world's first satellite, and some agricultural and industrial exhibits. The Americans clearly outdid them by sending a geodesic dome, automobiles, a swimming pool, and a 1,400 square-foot fully-equipped and furnished ranch house—the "All-State Typical American Home."

The house was to be shipped and trucked to Moscow's Sokolniki Park as a collection of two-by-fours, drywall, plywood, screws, nails, paint, and the tools to put it all together. The carpets, furniture, bookcases, pictures, and *tchotchkes* would be provided by Macy's, who would also be represented at the fair.

```
                            FACT SHEET

                  All-State Typical American Home

    SIZE OF HOUSE: 44 by 36 feet, including 10-foot wide walkway through
    the middle which is for display purposes and would not be included
    in a house designed to be lived in.  Patio extends 12 feet on one
    side.

    LIVING AREA: 1,144 square feet, excluding walkway and patio.

    TYPE OF HOUSE: one-story ranch, contemporary style.

    ROOMS: 6 rooms -- living room, kitchen, dining room, 3 bedrooms and
    a bath and a half.

    PRICE IN U.S.A.: The same house could be duplicated anywhere in the
    United States for $11,000 to $13,000, exclusive of land.

    The identical house is on sale for $14,490, including a quarter-acre
    of land, as one of six models at the All-State community at Commack,
    Long Island, N. Y.  Other models range from $13,990 to $17,290 at
    All-State at Commack.  This home can be bought at Commack under FHA
    or VA financing.  A veteran could buy it for as little as $101 monthly
    carrying charges without a down payment on a 30-year mortgage.

    BUILDER: All-State Properties, Inc., of Floral Park, Long Island,
    N. Y., Herbert Sadkin, president.  A publicly-owned real estate and
    home building firm which is currently developing five communities
    on Long Island, N. Y.; a 5,000-home community at the newly-created
    city of Lauderhill, Fla., near Fort Lauderdale; at Louisville, Ky.,
    and a Maryland suburb of Washington, D. C.  Owns controlling interest
    in Montauk Beach Company, Inc., which includes the Montauk Manor
    hotel and lodge and 3,100 acres of land on the easternmost tip of
    Long Island.

    FURNISHINGS AND DECORATIONS: Macy's New York from regular stock at a
    total cost of less than $5,000.

    KITCHEN: All-electric kitchen by General Electric Company.

    HEATING: Warm-Air heating system provided by the Labor-Management
    Industry Fund of the Sheet Metal Workers Union Local #55, fired by a
    gas furnace from General Electric Company.

    BATHROOM: Fixtures by AllianceWare, Inc., and tile by United States
    Ceramic Tile Co.

    TYPE OF CONSTRUCTION: Wood frame, with 13,802 board feet of lumber
    contributed by General Lumber Company.

    ARCHITECT: Stanley H. Klein of Jamaica, N. Y.

    EXTERIOR WALLS: vertical wood siding in natural redwood finish,
    random width, and plywood siding, vertical batten pattern, painted
    light yellow.  All paint contributed by Paxon Paint Co.

    ROOF: low-pitch, gabled; white asphalt shingles for roofing and
    white wood shingles for gables.

    EXTERIOR OPENINGS: sliding aluminum windows in all rooms except
    living room, which has triple window unit, combination fixed sash and
    awning type; 2 sets of aluminum sliding doors in living room and
    dining room opening onto patio; flush entrance door, painted cobalt
    blue.  Aluminum windows and doors contributed by Bennel Co., Inc.
```

Part of a well-used Fact Sheet for the All-State Typical American Home.

All-State Properties, the real estate development company I worked for in 1959, built housing developments on Long Island. The owner was preparing to go public and make it a national entity. He was intrigued to learn that the State Department was planning to sponsor a trade fair in Russia and that the organizers were looking for a builder who could supply them with a house. Levitt & Sons (think Levittown), at the time the largest residential builder in the United States, had turned the project down.

Billy, whose public relations company had deep political connections, was the one who brought the deal to my boss. This would be an expensive undertaking, since the builder would have to bear the costs, but in return would get a lot of publicity out of it.

"If we go through with this," I heard my boss say, "I want our name on the front page of *The New York Times!*"

"Guaranteed!" was the response he got from Tex McCrary, the PR company's owner and Billy's boss. McCrary's clients were some of New York's political heavyweights.

This was the plan: the house was to be "a typical American home." Our company had built a ranch house design with great success in many communities on Long Island. To start, we would construct a model version of the ranch house we had built with great success in many communities on Long Island. The model would be staged in the parking lot of the largest shopping center on Long Island: Roosevelt Field, near Garden City. We announced that this was the house that was going to Moscow, and it was open for public viewing. Roosevelt Field was also a great location to pick up some sales for houses in our projects.

Because many Russians would be visiting the house in Moscow, we needed an easy way for them to move through it, see all the rooms, and leave. So, our designers split the house in half and opened up the walls facing the interior walkway. People were able to walk through the middle of the house and view the layout on both the left and right. This worked well in the shopping center model house and it eventually did in Moscow, too.

Russia had just launched Sputnik, and Billy brilliantly tried to name our house the Splitnik. But the State Department would not let us use the name; they clearly didn't find it as funny as we did and it probably would not have gone over well with the Russians. Billy continued to use the moniker but we were careful to avoid saying it on the building site in Russia.

Previewing the model house at the shopping center gave us the opportunity to delineate all the parts and pieces required to rebuild it in Russia. One of my responsibilities was to coordinate the construction of the house on Long Island and serve as the company's representative. Our vice president of construction would then take four New York City union construction workers to Moscow to build the house for the show's opening on July 25, 1959.

Vice President Richard Nixon was to open the fair in Moscow and visit the exhibits with Premier Nikita Khrushchev. We were told that the two were scheduled to tour the house the day before the show opened to the Russian public, and that all the major media organizations would cover the event. Nixon and Khrushchev would be in the house for about five minutes. This was pretty good publicity for a company about to go public, and our announcement would be coordinated with the Nixon-Khrushchev visit.

About two weeks before the construction vice president and crew were due to depart, I was asked to come into my boss's office. The executive staff were there, as was Billy and some people from his office. As I entered the conference room everyone beamed at me with welcoming smiles. This was not normal. I immediately felt uncomfortable and needed to go to the bathroom. I was told that the construction VP was *not* taking the crew to Moscow, and that instead, I was.

Me? Going to Moscow to build a house? "You guys are kidding me. Ha ha."

They were not kidding. I was the only project manager familiar with what we had built in the parking lot of the Long Island shopping center. I was to go, and in two short weeks. There was much scrambling around to get my passport, work visa, and necessary documents.

Why the construction vice president backed down from this plum assignment was never discussed, but we thought it might have been because his parents were Russian-born and may have come to the U.S. without proper papers. He could have thought that he would be taken hostage or something like that. If I knew then that my mother came to the U.S. at age 16 with a forged passport from what at the time was Russia (later to become Lithuania), maybe I would have worried, too.

I was elated, nervous, and disappointed. I had promised my bride of eight months that we would go on our postponed honeymoon as soon as my construction of the model house in the shopping center was completed. Now I would need to revise my honeymoon promise—maybe meeting in Paris after the Russia gig wouldn't be so bad.

The newlyweds.

The makings of the house had been loaded on a ship for Finland and were then to be trucked to Moscow. I needed time on the job site to coordinate with the Russians, as they were going to supply us with workers to assist in the construction. And I was told that the slab foundation, based on our plans, would already be installed by the time we arrived.

No worries.

2 LOUIE AND THE COFFEE BREAK

Departing Idlewild (aka JFK) Airport, my wife and brother in the middle saying farewell.

My construction crew and I left the United States on June 19, 1959, to go build the house in Moscow. The crew was made up of the lead carpenter, Odd Siqueland; the trim carpenter, John Petrocelli; the drywall finisher, George Hartman; and the painter, Louis Epstein. Louis, who we always called Louie, was born in Russia and fluent in the language, but we decided to keep that a secret.

George and Louie on the Aeroflot plane to Russia.

John and Odd on the Aeroflot plane to Russia.

I understood that the New York City building trade unions agreed that these four men could do rough and finish carpentry, drywall, and painting. The unions even allowed the crew to install the sinks and water closet, but with the strict proviso that these were non-operating fixtures. If we were in NYC, this project would have involved about five different unions. The Russians would install the electrical system.

Construction crew in Brussels on layover to Russia.
[from left] Louie, George, John *[behind]*, Odd.

After a long flight from New York to Brussels, we enjoyed some famous Belgian beer while waiting for our Moscow-bound Russian plane. Once onboard, it appeared that the Aeroflot pilot was military-trained, so all of the plane's maneuvers were brusque and without consideration for human cargo. We were fed our boiled chicken dinner on heavy china that spent more time on our laps and the floor than on our pull-down trays.

The crew and me *[in shades]* on layover in Brussels airport.
Photo taken by John with my camera.

The sky was clear, and I wanted to take pictures of the expansive landscape of mountains and forest beneath the plane. I removed the camera from my pack and held it up to the small window, but I was immediately set upon by a solidly-built stewardess who told me, as she held my arm in a steel grip, that photos were not allowed because we were flying over Russian territory.

I had been so caught up in my responsibilities and preparing for this adventure that I'd had little time to digest what was really happening. Now it hit me. *Holy shit. Are you kidding me? I'm on a plane going to Russia. I'm going to supervise the building of a house, which is on a ship in thousands of pieces. The completion of this house is going to launch my employer's march to national prominence and financial success. On top of this, the vice president of the United States and the premier of the Soviet Union will be my guests.*

I took a tour of my confidence level:

Build a house? *I've done that, but always near a lumberyard where I can get the material I need.*

Supervise four senior-level New York City construction workers away from home? *I must maintain my authority and keep them happy.*

In Russia? *I guess I'll find out.*

It felt like I was about to get dumped in the water, so the only thing to do was swim! I started breathing heavily and wondered if it was a dream or a nightmare.

Reality shook me out of this anxiety as we landed in Moscow. We were met by a U.S. embassy official who would make sure we got our luggage and tools.

Items were shipped in a variety of wooden containers.

Our tools were packed in a large wooden crate, which was designed so that we could detect if it had been opened for inspection. It hadn't, which surprised us, as the box was large enough to contain a table saw, chop saw, and many sets of electric and hand tools. It could have also contained tools of the spy trade and even a small fold-up plane, but that was not why we were in Russia.

We were taken to our hotel to unload and then on to the embassy for our briefing. Unbelievable. This is the Cold War. We are in Moscow, Russia. Suddenly I realized that the U.S. missiles pointing in my direction… are ours!

Construction projects away from home require certain necessary comforts that were not readily available in Russia. You want your morning coffee break, your afternoon cold beer, and your dirty clothes laundered. For us, each of these necessities required innovative efforts and nose-to-nose negotiations that sometimes resulted in hilarious outcomes.

After a couple of days of indoctrination and touristy things, we opened the tool crate and started laying out the floor plan in anticipation of the delivery of all the parts of our house. They had been shipped to Finland and put on trucks for delivery to Sokolniki Park, where the event was being staged. The two concrete slabs, which the Russians had installed, had their problems but we were able to work around them (more about that later).

Our lead carpenter, Odd, could have cared less that he was in the Soviet Union working on a history-making project. As far as he was concerned, he could have been banging nails in the Bronx. Mid-morning of our first day at the site, Odd approached me and wanted to know when the coffee wagon would arrive. "Are you kidding me?" was my response. "This is Russia. They don't do coffee. This is tea-in-a-glass country, and they have no idea what a coffee wagon is. You'll have to wait for lunch. Take a water break instead."

He wasn't happy, and I didn't want our relationship to get off to a bad start. I thought that I would visit some of the other exhibit sites to see what they were doing about break time. Apparently, a snack bar was to have opened to provide American-style food, but it wasn't ready.

Odd Siqueland, the lead carpenter.

Odd wasn't satisfied with my pushing him off. I was intent on maintaining my alpha dog status, and he was nipping at my heels. He took a little red book out of his pocket and showed me a union rule clearly stating that "management must provide a 15-minute break at mid-morning and afternoon." He was not open to my explanation that "coffee break" didn't necessarily mean coffee and that he could take a break, but there just wasn't any coffee available. He insisted and threatened, "We are going to strike!"

I was stunned. If we were in New York, I would have put Odd on the next subway home and filed a report with his union rep. But I took his threat seriously enough to gather the remaining three men on our crew to work out a solution.

In 1959 in an urban park in the middle of Moscow, what were our resources?

Louie!

Louie, our Russian-speaking painter, was thrust into the dilemma. I gave him a handful of rubles and told him to find a cab and come back with coffee. Period.

"Louie," I said, "you are going to make history by establishing the first coffee break in Russia, so don't come back without coffee." He fully understood the challenge and was visibly excited to accomplish this important mission.

"Don't verrrry boss, I'll be rrrright beck."

The men agreed that this was our best approach, and they convinced Odd to put the union rules away and wait for Louie to return. He grudgingly agreed, so we went back to work and waited... and waited... and waited.

We had lunch and waited some more.

By midafternoon, I was concerned that Louie might actually not be coming back.

At about 3 p.m., a cab pulled up and Louie hopped out carrying a large cardboard box. He set it down as we approached and took out five glass jars of coffee and a bag of the best cinnamon buns I have ever tasted.

I hugged Louie and told Odd that if he complained that the coffee was cold (it was), he would be on the next plane to New York.

Louie never revealed what he had done, but here is my best guess: he went to a food market and bought five jars of jam and somehow emptied them and washed out the jars. He took them to a restaurant or one of the embassies and got the coffee, stopped at a bakery, and returned to the site. He told us to save the jars because he had arranged for coffee to be brought to us every morning. I think he attempted to arrange something with the cab driver who was probably going to get a piece of the profits.

It never happened. Within a few days, the park commissary finally opened to all of the U.S. construction workers who were working on the various buildings and exhibits for the exposition. Of course, they served coffee.

[from left] Russian-speaking American guide, John, and George eating at the commissary.

For us, the food situation was terrible. Because we were Americans, we were restricted to stay within a designated zone in Moscow that contained mostly hotels and very few restaurants. Unfortunately, every place we went had the same menu and the same bland, boring, beige food.

Someone told me about a Chinese restaurant in a hotel that housed the many Chinese businesspeople who visited Moscow. We all anticipated the change in cuisine, but the restaurant's menu was in

Chinese and we couldn't find a waiter who could speak English. We were just about ready to leave when Louie stood up from the table and said, "I'll be rrrright beck."

He walked over to a Chinese waiter, and they seemed to be having a conversation. We were amazed. After a short time, he returned and told us he had ordered a variety of dishes that would be coming to our table in a few minutes. We were all perplexed as to how this could happen.

I said to Louie, jokingly, "Do you speak Chinese?"

"Rrrright, boss," was his reply.

In his heavy Eastern European Yiddish accent, Louie explained that when his family was driven out of Russia during the Bolshevik Revolution, instead of going west, his family and others from their *shtetl* went east and settled in China. Louie was a child at the time and grew up in an immigrant Jewish community in Shanghai speaking Chinese, Yiddish, and Russian.

Russian cab driver and Louie discuss life in Russia.

Louie *[second from right]* with Russian workers.

Louie loved to visit Chinese restaurants in Brooklyn and have conversations with the waiters and cooks that blew the minds of his friends.

Louie was kicked off the project and sent home just as we were wrapping things up.

One day I noticed a Russian military officer hanging around our job site. He seemed to have a particular interest in what we were doing. Our house was located at the outer edge of the exhibit site and near a roadway that was closed off during construction. We were surrounded by a high temporary fence and protected from unwelcome visitors.

This military guy hovered outside the fence for the greater part of the day.

The next morning, I received an oral message that a U.S. embassy official wanted to talk to me. This was not unusual, as we had been told that any matters that might affect our relationship with our Russian hosts would be handled in a confidential "in the street" manner. That literally meant that we were to meet away from the embassy and somewhere in the park.

I had first encountered this kind of communication when we arrived at the embassy to have what we called our "Russian indoctrination." While our crew was taken on a tour of the facilities, I was ushered outside by a U.S. embassy attaché who told me what to look out for, how to behave, and all sorts of basic things to be aware of, such as not wandering off beyond the area of our hotel. When I asked him why we were talking while strolling on the sidewalk, he said that the Russians could hear much of what was said within the walls of our embassy.

"Hold on," I chirped incredulously. "That's our property."

"Yes," he replied. "But they built it."

He assured me that there were "safe" rooms where the real work took place.

I was to experience this method of communication a number of times, including when I fired our Russian construction workers, but that didn't happen until we started building the house.

Back to Louie. The embassy official told me that the military guy who had been hanging around was Louie's brother. Evidently, they hadn't seen each other for many years but had kept in contact. Part of Louie's family had not gone to China, which really complicated Louie's story in the Chinese restaurant.

It turns out Louie had been followed out of the park by a U.S. embassy employee. It seems that our government was doing its due diligence by keeping an eye on our construction workers whose away-from-home behavior might not make us look good.

Louie seems to have met up with his brother when he was shopping for our coffee break and, according to the U.S. embassy attaché, Louie was observed at a later time to be giving his brother a large amount of money and a suitcase of clothing. Clothing was more valuable than cash on the Russian black market. The embassy official told me that the Russians did not know about Louie's transgressions.

The next morning, he was on the plane to Brussels and back to New York.

Before he left, I spoke with Louie. He had expected the outcome. It was near the end of the project by this time, and his construction work was basically finished: he was hanging pictures and working with the Macy's decorating team.

He told me his brother had changed his name before his military career began. Being Jewish in the Soviet Union in the 1950s was not a very friendly situation. Being Jewish *and* being in the military was unheard of.

Louie's brother had come to the site because he was being relocated and he wanted to say goodbye to his brother.

John, Louie, and George with constant crowd of onlookers standing behind the fence.

3 COLD BEER AND LAUNDRY

Waiting line at the Kremlin to view bodies of Stalin and Lenin.

Now that the coffee break was established to begin the day, cold beer was needed to end the day. The streetscape in Moscow in 1959 was bleak and bare. Of course, convenient New York-style bodegas did not exist; there was no place we could get a six-pack.

When we first checked in to the hotel, we had been introduced to our "in-tourist guide," who would be my contact outside of the exhibit area. He told us where we could go, and where we couldn't go. He made sure that we jumped to the head of the long (obligatory) lines to view the bodies of Lenin and Stalin. He was fluent in English and was constantly preaching about how great Russia was, how all of the people were working and living comfortably, and all of their children were being educated.

I asked him where we could get some cold beer. He told me that Russian beer was the best and because of the high-quality ingredients and special processing, it didn't need to be refrigerated. After he gave us a short lecture on the differences between communism and capitalism, he concluded with: "Refrigeration is capitalistic tool!"

He pretty much zeroed in on me and invited me to experience some of the Soviet efficiencies and advanced technologies that made life easier for the people. My cold beer request was ignored.

"We will proceed to the Metro and I will demonstrate what the communist doctrine can produce," he proudly proclaimed as we left the hotel.

He took me to Moscow's subway system, some parts of which had originally been built to double as air-raid shelters. The older stations were quite decorative with handsome wall coverings and crystal chandeliers. The newer, outlying stations were not as elaborate.

As we descended the stairs to a main Metro station, he looked up at me and said, checking his watch: "When we reach the bottom of the stairs, the train will arrive exactly on schedule." Given that I had spent much of my life in New York City waiting for the subway, I looked forward to this remarkable achievement.

The station platform was virtually empty with a scattering of people gazing at the works of art and the elaborate lighting. But there was no train.

Minutes went by and my guide kept looking down the track for the hint of a moving light coming toward us. More minutes went by. He was getting uncomfortable, constantly checking his watch and the tracks. After seven or eight minutes, he was in a frenzy.

In a rage, he turned to me and at the top of his voice said a couple of things in Russian, as his face kept changing color. I could not understand a word, but it was clear by his flying arms and his bulging eyes that there were two things on his mind. My interpretation of what he might have said goes something like this:

He started by yelling "America has racial issues!" Then he cooled down and moved into a nasty smirk, "and *we* conquered space before you did!"

Then he turned and ran up the stairs. I never saw him again.

I don't remember if I ended up taking the train. I probably just left the station because at that time I did not want to risk ending up outside of the approved zone.

We did, however, get our beer, and it *was* cold.

View from the steps of the Leningradsky Hotel.

A few days after getting to know some of the hotel workers, I discovered the real reason we hadn't been getting cold beer. There was an ample supply of beer in the hotel restaurant, but there weren't enough refrigerators for both beer and food. The chef, who I gave some rubles to with the request, "We would like the beer to be cold, maybe this will help," told me that they had to throw away much of their fresh food because cold storage was very limited, but he assured me that he could squeeze some bottles into the meat cooler.

Hot coffee and cold beer. Life was beginning to settle in. Now we needed to make sure our work clothes were kept laundered.

Every day we needed a clean set of work clothes and we were promised that the hotel would be happy to provide this service. That was good news because asking Odd to wash his undies in the bathtub would probably violate some union rule.

After the first couple of days, we left our soiled stuff in the designated space and anticipated their fresh return within a reasonable period of time. Our daily routine was to come back to the hotel after the work day, clean up, change into clean clothes, and gather in my room for cold beer and small talk before dinner. (As the foreman of the project, I was assigned a private room; the rest of the crew doubled up in two rooms.)

At the end of the first week as we were enjoying our beer, I asked, "Are you guys comfortable? How are your rooms working out? Any problems with hotel services?"

John said that he was running out of fresh work clothes and had been waiting for his laundry to be returned clean. I told him I would check into this in the morning.

As we finished our beer and left my room to go down to the restaurant, we passed John and Louie's room and saw their bag of laundry at their door. "That's nice," I said. "Our timing was right not to complain."

The next evening while we were reviewing the day, I asked everyone if they had fresh towels, as mine had been removed and not returned. Everyone said they were okay. I mentioned that I would run down to the desk and try to get a towel so I could wash up.

I was finishing my beer and getting ready to leave when there was a knock on my door. It was a maid bearing fresh towels.

Four sets of eyebrows were raised with the same thought. So, for the next few afternoons while having our beer and during our regular conversation, we would bring things up: "I don't have any soap." "I could use another washcloth." "My trash basket is full." Within minutes of these complaints, there would be a knock on the door and our requests would be answered.

Soviet room service at its best.

We decided that we did not want to play this game any longer and that we would look for the hidden listening device. We did not intend to destroy it, just to verify it.

We looked in the obvious places, assuming that the Russians had seen the same spy movies we did: the lamps, the moldings, behind the pictures, under the drawers. We finally found it hardwired in the telephone mouthpiece. If we removed it, we assumed it would just be replaced, so we agreed to say swell things about our hosts and save the complaints for the job site.

The U.S. embassy attaché told me that there was a 10 p.m. curfew, at which time the hotel doors would be locked. If you were found locked out and on the street, you could face arrest.

Another interesting warning was that we were not allowed to be in the presence of a Soviet woman unattended. If this happened and you were caught, he had said, you could be "detained for a period of nine months to ensure that the woman was not pregnant." I reminded him that a full nine-month period was not necessary to determine pregnancy. He said he knew that, but apparently the Russians didn't.

The program from the famous Russian clown (Oleg) Popov's performance with a local circus.

Later in the month, we heard a story about a Russian-speaking construction worker from Texas who had spent the evening alone with a young Russian woman and arrived at our hotel well after the curfew. He found an unlocked door, which led to the back stairs of the hotel. When he got to the third floor, there was a partition wall and a closed door on the landing. He opened the door and walked into a large room with many men sitting at desks with earphones: our room-service operators.

He was immediately grabbed, and as he was about to be hustled back out in the street to a waiting police car, he asked the person in charge how he should answer the authorities when they asked how he got into the room.

He indicated to his handlers that it might be uncomfortable for everybody if it was discovered that he was able to walk through two unlocked doors.

The next morning, he was on a plane to Brussels.

Setting aside all this intrigue and supported with the comforts of coffee, cold beer, and clean work clothes, we were in good spirits to keep moving ahead on our house.

4 THE FUR HAT AND BENNY GOODMAN

GUM Department store across Red Square from the Kremlin.

Before I left the U.S., I had promised my mother that I would bring back authentic Russian fur hats for our family. I asked around, and someone suggested that I go to the GUM department store on Red Square, right across from the Kremlin's mausoleum, which at the time housed the waxy-looking corpses of Joseph Stalin and Vladimir Lenin.

GUM is an impressive structure built in the late 1890s and is what we would consider a shopping mall. There is a wide promenade with stores on either side opened to strolling shoppers. On the upper level, more shops are accessed by a balcony that looks over the lower walkway. This level contained specialty stores, which were, at that time, accessible only to the upper echelons of Russian society. The

The Kremlin wall.

length of the building is 800 feet, and the ceiling is a vaulted iron-and-glass structure with a diameter of 48 feet. In 1959, this ceiling was considered one of the great wonders of construction engineering with 20,000 panes of glass held in place by 50,000 metal pods or frames. This 740-ton ceiling was made to support the heavy snow loads that accumulate in Russian winters.

This shopping mall differed from what we had in the United States. There were no glitzy signs or displays or fancy storefronts exhibiting what was on sale within. There were no chain stores or department stores. If you wanted to buy shoes, you went to the shoe store; if you wanted to buy coats, you went to the coat store.

I wanted fur hats, so I went to the hat store.

The Moscow River.

I arrived with the excited anticipation of being able to choose from different styles and different furs. I was in the country where fur hats come from—the original source. I wanted to get silver lamb for my Mom and maybe black bear for my Dad and brothers. My wife would like mink or beaver (this was years before I decided that the only fur I would take from animals would be the kind of fur that grows back).

The store had bins full of many varieties of hats and caps. I did not see any fur hats; these hats were mostly made of wool or synthetic fabrics. I asked the clerk to see the fur hats, anticipating that they were kept in a special display. "We don't have fur hats," the clerk said in almost perfect English with a bit of a sarcastic overtone. I was surprised, disappointed, and puzzled.

"I know this is summer and people aren't wearing fur hats and they're just not being displayed, right?" I hoped.

"We don't have fur hats," she repeated.

"But I've seen pictures of Russians with fur hats. It's part of your heritage. It's part of your culture," I begged.

She responded again as she looked down at the bins of fake fur hats and repeated: "We don't have fur hats."

I wondered about the possible reasons why the largest store in Russia didn't have fur hats. Maybe it's summer and they don't stock them. Maybe people actually go out and kill animals and make their own fur hats. No. Something was wrong here.

The sales clerk fully understood what I was asking for. Her attitude was standoffish, and she seemed as bothered by my asking as I was bothered by her reply. I tried to discuss my dilemma with her, but she would not engage. I asked her if she had a fur hat that kept her head warm in the winter. I tried to be charming. I asked her if she saw people in Moscow in winter wearing fur hats.

I fired questions at her, but she remained tight-lipped. I think I was starting to upset her, so I told her I would go away if she could tell me how I could get a fur hat. "You go to the district," she said.

"The district? What and where is that?" I questioned.

She turned and walked away.

Okay. That was the Russian game—hide and seek, scavenger hunt. Call it what you may, I'm in. I hailed a cab and asked the driver, "Do you understand English?"

"*Da,*" he answered.

"Take me to the district... *puzalesta,*" I directed him with a "please" in Russian.

The Russian language is wonderful. It's fun to pronounce a word that rarely comes out understandable. And it's complicated, such as having two words for blue, one that describes dark blueberry blue, and one that's more for robin's egg blue.

One of the more upscale Moscow neighborhoods in our "zone."

The cab drove through a part of Moscow that was far outside of our designated zone. The area felt older, European, with tree-lined, single-lane streets with two- and three-story buildings that were well-preserved. This was in contrast to most of the postwar construction I had seen which consisted of bland, concrete buildings without design features. These buildings were definitely prewar.

Some of the buildings had storefronts; no signs, just large windows and glass doors… and in those large windows were female mannequins like the ones in store windows on Fifth Avenue in New York City. They were dressed the same way, in the latest Fifth Avenue and Parisian styles.

I was stunned. No *babushkas* here. These mannequins were not made in the images of the classically Rubenesque Russian women I had seen on the streets and in the parks of our designated zone. These were sleek, tall, and very French. I was even more astonished when I saw what looked like these fashionable, svelte mannequins coming to life emerging from large black Russian cars and entering the stores. Who were these elegant people? Where were the *babushka-*wearing somber-faced women I had encountered up to now?

It didn't take long for me to figure what this was all about. Like many, I had been fooled into believing that Russia was basically a single-class society and that everyone shared equally. The people on this street, in this district, were the elite, the special few, the politically advantaged who it seemed were being served by the rest of the population. It was a division of class that wasn't supposed to exist.

I felt embarrassingly naïve. I wasn't going to support this. I told the driver to take me back to my hotel. The fur hats were not going to be gifts I would bring home.

Billboards at street level in Moscow.

After a couple of weeks in Moscow, I became resolved in my new understanding that Russia was not anywhere close to being the dream of Lenin or even the boisterous rhetoric of Khrushchev. It was clearly a two-class society with the power in the hands of the governing body.

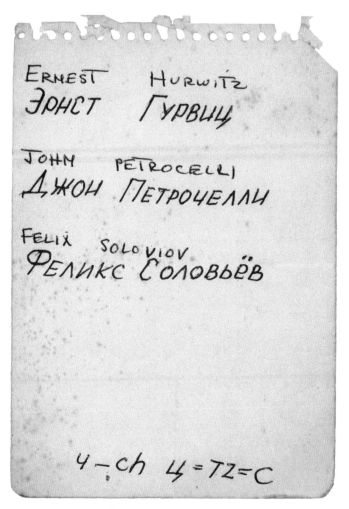

Crew names with translation.

Another incident brought this to light. A fellow American who was also there working on the exhibition mentioned that the best food in town was served at a hotel a few blocks from where we were staying but was outside of our designated zone. He said not to worry about the restricted area situation, that no one was really checking. What he said about "no one checking" was not really true, but we were willing to try—because we had figured out the system.

When we had first arrived in Moscow, the American embassy representative informed us that we were not free to wander all over Moscow and that we were restricted to a designated area. We were given maps with shaded areas indicating our "no go" zone. We could walk only around the touristy areas and some neighborhoods near our hotel.

One night early in our visit, we decided to take an evening stroll within the designated area. We noticed that we were being followed by a guy in a black raincoat who was in turn being trailed by a slowly moving black car that stayed about a half a block behind him. It was June and warm, and most of the people in the street wore brightly-colored short sleeve shirts and even sandals. This guy stuck out like coal in a snowdrift. He was the Russian version of the Pink Panther (we should have called him the Red Panther).

We were uncomfortable with this and decided to let him know that we were aware of his presence so that maybe he would leave us alone. So, we came up with a plan.

One evening we left the hotel and split up into two groups. Louie and I were in the first group; George, John, and Odd were in the other. Our plan was that the group not being followed would circle around the block and come up behind this guy and his trailing vehicle.

It worked perfectly. He followed Louie and me. He probably knew that I was the highest-ranking person in the group, that Louie spoke and understood Russian, and that we would be the most likely ones to leave the designated zone.

Typical Moscow neighborhood.

Louie and I turned the corner and slowed down until the rest of the crew caught up. We turned to see George, John, and Odd passing the black car and getting close to our target.

We turned around, circling the guy, and all said "BOO!" at the same time.

The man gazed at us with a blank expression, walked out of our circle, and got into the waiting black car. We never saw him again and felt assured, after closely watching the people around us, that we had permanently lost our tail.

We were excited about our newly won freedom and felt confident about crossing over into the restricted area. We agreed that it seemed like an acceptable risk: if we got caught we would be asked to leave and told not wander from our designated zone again. Our courage for breaking the rules was bolstered by the anticipation of a good meal.

The recommended place was the Hotel Ukraina. It was set back about 100 yards from the sidewalk in an open plaza. As we turned into the walkway leading to the front door, we could see two very large uniformed soldiers standing on each side of the entrance door with rifles at their sides. As we got closer, they got bigger and we got slower. Their eyes were fixed on the five of us as we approached.

I told my four partners to relax. "Don't make eye contact. Act as if you are going into the hotel and keep looking at the door." They agreed but not with great enthusiasm.

"They're not going to shoot us," I assured them. "The worst thing that could happen is that they won't let us enter," I boldly said, barely believing it myself.

There were three steps leading to the double door entrance with a soldier on each side. As I approached the first step, I noticed that my companions had drifted back a bit and that I was alone. Suddenly the guards snapped into a salute and opened both doors while standing at attention. We moved quickly inside.

We exhaled with relief, then gasped at what we walked into: the sound of music, a warm murmur of conversation, and the greeting of a very jovial *maître d'* who was right out of central casting. The setting was a perfect 19th-century time warp.

We were greeted as if we had been expected and were ushered into a huge dining room, the kind where you walk down three steps to enter and are usually watched by the room's occupants as you descend. However, no one was looking at us because they were very busy dining and dancing to live music under magnificent crystal chandeliers.

The band was right out of a 1930s Bing Crosby movie with about 15 musicians in white tuxedos playing American Songbook swing music. I remained stunned as we were ushered to our table two tiers above the dance floor. Three waiters appeared and started popping and pouring champagne into crystal glasses.

The only conversation between my crew was variations on, "Can you believe this?"

Postcard of a fancy Moscow hotel, circa 1959.

The *maître d'* came to our table and said, in a deep Continental accent, that he was honored to have us in his restaurant and that we simply needed to relax and enjoy our visit.

The expression "wined and dined" was made very clear to us as we were brought course after course of American-style cuisine. The steaks were perfect and the desserts bordered on exceptional. The truth is that we were drinking so much really good champagne that there might have been a distortion to our high ratings. And not to forget that we had not eaten this kind of rich food in many days.

During one of the pauses between courses, I went to the bandstand to look at the sheet music these guys were playing. It was pure swing and beautifully orchestrated. I walked around to the rear of the trumpet section and saw that each musician had a tattered book of music that contained arrangements of familiar tunes by Glenn Miller, Tommy Dorsey, Benny Goodman, Charlie Barnet, and Duke Ellington. The book was published by Belwin-Mills Publishing Corp. of Melville, N.Y. The freedom of American jazz had permeated the Russian culture, and during the Cold War it was thought to play a vital role in turning many young Soviet minds to the freedom that existed in the U.S.

The music playing in the dining room was slow swing and mostly the two-step classics that I grew up with. The dance floor was crowded with designer-dressed women and their male partners who were much duller in their dark blue military dress or black suits.

I returned to our table and sampled some of the after-dinner drinks that put us all in a very happy, well-stuffed mood. The *maître d'* came over and asked if we had enjoyed our evening and if he could bring anything else. I said that we were extremely satisfied and asked if he would send our compliments to the chef and the kitchen staff.

In an attempt to impress him with one of the few French phrases I knew, I requested, *"L'addition, s'il vous plait?"*

"No, no, no you must not pay. You are my guest. You are guests of the Russian government. We are honored that you have visited us tonight." We all shook hands and hugged as we were escorted out through the elaborate lobby.

I guess no one had told them we were well outside of our designated zone.

Hotel restaurant receipts.

It was obvious that our fellow diners were the movers and shakers of Russian society. The men in the business suits were high-ranking politicos or party members. Actually, we had learned that you couldn't be a politician if you weren't an active member of the Communist party. Engineers, doctors, and other professionals would not be allowed to practice their profession without loyalty to the party.

These were the guys who could afford to dress their ladies in the latest Paris fashions. These were the guys who could afford the real fur hats.

In the structure of the Russian population, the next group in descending order were the officers and members of the "trusts." These were the bosses and supervisors in the factories and at the farms. They might be called the middle class, but they were few in number and would not be allowed in the Hotel Ukraina.

From what I saw, the rest of the population, the majority of Russians, didn't seem too happy.

What I ended up taking back to my family were some beautifully crafted wooden boxes, together with my newly acquired maturity about how some of the rest of the world lives.

5 THE DOM AND THE CROSSTOWN TRIP

Matchbook from the American House Club.

The American embassy in Moscow had a uniformed U.S. military attachment assigned to protect its property and its inhabitants. The squad consisted of the Army, Navy, and Marines. In 1959, these servicemen had a rough time. With the U.S. and Russia in a cold war and the unfriendly attitude of the Russian government, our men in uniform were burdened with many restrictions that affected their off-duty social life. In reality, however, being sent to Moscow for a military assignment was a plum gig for these young, virile, professional servicemen. Here's why.

The Amerikanski Dom, aka the American House, was a sprawling mansion on the Moscow River and was considered part of the American embassy even though it was in a different part of town. The Dom was open to the working staff of other countries' embassies located in Moscow but off-limits to the Russians. It was, in effect, the U.S. military's playpen.

Two nights a week the Dom was open to all, so long as you were not Russian. Passports were required. There was a huge bar that served all the liquor and beer that any upscale American bar would provide. There was a large lounge with overstuffed chairs and couches, and the most recent American pop music playing on a state-of-the-art sound system. They didn't serve much food, just bar snacks such as peanuts and pretzels.

The bar and the lounge were open to visitors during these two nights, but the rest of the Dom was not. One night a week was movie night, and you had to be invited by a serviceman. The movie shown would be the same current flick that was being seen by Americans in their local theaters. The other nights of the week were saved for what we called private party time.

The military overseers of the Dom would invite staff of the other embassies for social gatherings. Because the U.S. military contingent was primarily made up of men, the invitations generally went to female staff members.

The people in the other international embassies experienced the same restrictions on their personal movement as the Americans did, but the Dom more than helped to alleviate this problem. There were no restrictions on those private party nights, and you only have to go to the near side of your imagination to figure out what went on inside the Dom.

This was the place the G.I.s could comfortably socialize, kick back, and relax. They also enjoyed the financial largesse of the Dom's activities. My scotch cost the same as it would have in New York City, but all of the liquor, beer, snacks, movies, and necessary supplies were donated by an American who (according to one of the bartenders) owned a chain of movie theaters and other businesses in the United States. These donations were his way of supporting the troops who served abroad. With all income and no expenses, the Dom was a cash cow for the military.

I was told by one military serviceman that his assignment would last for a year and that when he returned to the U.S. or to another assignment, he would have accumulated a large amount of cash. Besides having his military pay sent home, he would have acquired an additional five figures as his share of the profits from the Dom. It turns out that on their days off, the service men would work at the club and share all the profits. This made military assignments in Moscow much more palatable for these G.I.s.

Usually after our evening meal, my crew would call it a day, and I was free to roam. On the nights the Dom bar was open, I would take a short cab ride and join some of my fellow construction managers, mid-level diplomats, and other interesting international types for some conversation and an after-dinner drink or two. I was never invited to movie night or the party nights, but the couple of nights a week I did visit were enough to maintain my social skills.

One night I left the Dom and quickly found a cab to take me across town to my hotel. Cabs were easy to find as there were very few other cars on the street. I told the driver, in my best Russian, to take me to my hotel. Usually this direction was understood and I didn't need to repeat it or raise my voice like a good American.

The route from the Dom to my hotel was right through the center of Moscow, past Red Square, the GUM department store, and on to Gorky Street. Since I had taken this cab ride many times before, I took this opportunity to close my eyes to the not-very-exciting Moscow streetscape.

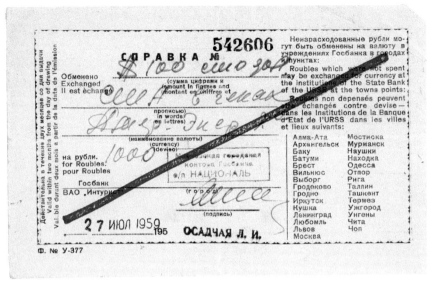

Currency exchange receipt.

I must have dozed off. My two-scotch limit would usually relax me, but not put me to sleep. When I opened my eyes and looked out the cab window, I saw farmland. No buildings, no wide streets with street lights, just dark land.

My first reaction was to notice that certain parts of my body were constricting. My next reaction was to assume that I was being kidnapped, but I quickly discounted this, since in all the kidnapping movies I had ever seen there are usually more than one kidnapper. The cab driver and I were alone in this swiftly moving vehicle, and he was small, happy, and old.

My next reaction was that he had taken a wrong turn and that we were lost. My last reaction was a very loud "HOLY #%@&! STOP THE CAB!" He turned to look at me and continued driving. He did not understand. I leaned up into his ear and shouted "STOP THE &@%#ING CAB!"

I thought I knew the word for "stop" in Russian. But what was it? Finally, he realized that something was wrong and he slowed down. Finally, I remembered *"Shtoy!"* Bingo, he stopped and turned around to face me. I realized that my bad Russian for "hotel" hadn't translated.

I was staying at the Hotel Leningrad, so when I got into the cab, I had said *"Chozeniska Leningradskya, pozhaluysta"* ("Hotel Leningrad, please," or at least that's what I thought I said). I didn't need two scotches to mispronounce that mouthful. It turns out that he was taking me to Leningrad, the city, which is 438 miles and a nine-hour drive from Moscow.

I looked at my watch. There was the 10 p.m. curfew at the hotel, at which point I would be locked out. We hadn't gone too far, but we needed to turn back right away. For the next few precious minutes, thanks to the use of hand signals and my extensive experience in playing charades, the driver understood the problem and the time constraint. He U-turned on two wheels while, I think, apologizing for not understanding me.

We must have been an inch from airborne when he came to a screeching stop at the Hotel Leningrad with a couple of minutes to spare. Thank goodness there was no traffic or traffic cops.

The taxi meter was in the high three figures and I included a generous tip. He refused the money indicating that it was his fault that we went the wrong way. We argued in our own languages while the nearby clock tower started chiming 10 times. I could just imagine him returning the cab to the garage without this fare. It was probably what he earned in a month, and my mispronunciation could have sent him to a gulag.

I took the money, threw it on the floor at the back of the cab, slammed the door, and ran into the hotel as the doors were being closed, yelling *"Spasiba!"* (Thank you!) over my shoulder.

On my way to my room I made two vows:

1. I've got to practice my Russian pronunciation; and

2. Maybe I should switch to one drink at the Dom.

6 FELIX, JAZZ, AND CHICKEN KIEV

Our first view of the house site and one of the concrete slabs on which it would be built.

During our first week in Russia, we visited the building site in Sokolniki Park. We were excited about the challenge ahead—bringing thousands of pieces of building material across the ocean and creating an exhibit house that thousands of Russians could visit, the same house that we had built hundreds of times for working-class families on Long Island.

But we were disappointed to find that the concrete slabs the house was going to be built on were really crappy, thanks to the poor quality of the concrete and the out-of-square dimension. These could potentially give us some problems later. The Russians had provided these slabs based on our plans and specifications, but the concrete was uneven and the aggregate exposed. It appeared to have been poured a couple of days before we arrived, although we were told that it had been done weeks ago. We could tell it was green (uncured). If this had taken place on Long Island, the contractor would have been required to remove and replace the slabs. But we didn't have a choice: we were in Russia, and we needed to work with what we had.

The Russian-built foundation slabs.

The first challenge was to figure out how to build our house on this foundation. I left this problem to my crew, confident they would resolve the issue.

In the meantime, I needed to find out where my house was. The site was bare except for the cement slabs and the large crate containing our tools. Someone on the site told me that the lumber, drywall, shingles, tile, cabinets, sinks, countertops, appliances, paint, nails, adhesive, and various parts had been offloaded from a ship in Finland and was currently being trucked to our site. I was directed to the materials staging area, where I was told to contact a Russian by the name of Felix, who was to be our logistics coordinator.

Exhibition logistics offices where I went for meetings with Felix.

Felix was normally in a happy state of mind, but he was serious about his responsibility to our project, and he was not in a happy mood when I met him. After I asked him about where our house was, he acknowledged that he was embarrassed because he couldn't give me any definite information about the whereabouts or arrival time of our materials. He was very frustrated, because he knew that we were ready to start construction.

In a more jovial tone and flawless English, he said, "This is not putting a shining light on Soviet efficiency." I could see that there was good chemistry between us and that we would have a friendly relationship.

Felix was a man of two distinct moods. When he was dealing with the responsibility of making sure our supplies were delivered, he was stern and demanding. When it was just the two of us or when he was with our crew, he was happy-go-lucky, always joking around, relaxed, and deeply concerned about our comfort and condition.

It was difficult for me to get any background on him. He never spoke about his family, and avoided discussing the quality of his life in the Soviet Union. He sidestepped my questions, and he wouldn't allow me to take his picture. I could tell that he struggled with not being able to open up to me to share his thoughts. He was, however, full of questions about my life in America, my family, my recent marriage, my new car, my education, and the kind of music I liked.

Roof truss parts arrive. These were sent from the U.S. by ship to Finland, then train to Moscow, then truck to site.

The first delivery of our materials finally made it to the site—not everything, but some of the main structural pieces, including all of the lumber that made up the roof trusses, the 2x4s that would frame the walls, the plywood sheathing, drywall, and all the fasteners and glue that held everything together. More was scheduled to come later;

there wasn't room for it all at one time, especially the appliances and Macy's furniture.

One day when we were in the park's transportation office trying to hunt down the location of our appliances, Felix flew into rage with one of the dispatchers who refused to tell him when the truck would arrive. As the loud, high-pitched conversation was in Russian, I was unable to understand what was being said, but suddenly Felix turned away and mumbled something under his breath that I did understand.

It was a Yiddish expletive that I was familiar with. As we left the office I said, "Felix, you said something in Yiddish. Are you Jewish?" He looked at me with an expression that to me said, "I can't answer that because my answer would get me into deep trouble with certain parties." From then on when we were together, Felix transmitted this unsaid message many times, knowing that I would understand.

[from right] Nikolai and fellow laborers sitting on drywall for the house.

Labor crew moves drywall into place, Nikolai in the middle.

I was totally unaware that being Jewish in the Soviet Union was a closely-held "let's not talk about it" subject. I thought all that had disappeared after World War II. In 1921, my parents left their home country of Lithuania because of the Bolsheviks and the rampant Jewish oppression. Apparently this repression, more subtle in 1959, still existed.

We ran into this attitude one sultry evening when my crew and I were strolling around our hotel after dinner. We wandered into a residential area and were taking in the sounds and smells of a working-class neighborhood. There were many people on the street, shopping and getting some air in a very peaceful setting. A group of very quiet and subdued people were gathered in front of one apartment building, most of them elderly. They seemed apprehensively waiting to enter. As we passed, I noticed that each person was clutching a book, and I could see that the book one woman was carrying had Hebrew letters on the cover. I stopped and asked Louie to find out if the woman was Jewish. He greeted her and asked, in both Russian and Yiddish, *"Puzhalsta. Do bienst a yid?"* ("Please. Are you Jewish?"). Angrily and in a hushed and hard voice, she responded, in Yiddish, *"Zall zin shah"* ("Quiet" or "shut up").

Typical day in Moscow Park—with an ice cream stand.

She and the rest of the group quickly filed into the building. After a short while, Louie and I realized that it was Friday night, the beginning of the Jewish Sabbath. They were not entering a synagogue, however; it was probably just someone's home.

Part of my close relationship with Felix was based on our shared love of jazz. I was surprised that he had such a deep knowledge about who was recording what and about major concerts in the United States. He actually knew about some of the jazz happenings in New York that I was unaware of. "Where are you getting all this information?" I asked him. "I'm really impressed and a bit surprised. I would expect that jazz is hands off behind the Iron Curtain."

"From the radio," Felix said.

"On the radio?" I questioned. "Do you have disc jockeys that play American jazz records?"

He looked at me as if we were talking about two different things. "Huh? Don't you know Warren Covington?"

"I know that he plays jazz on an international radio station that broadcasts into Europe."

"Yes," Felix said. "Voice of America. We listen every night."

Covington had been a jazz trombonist with the Jimmy Dorsey Orchestra and was now a folk hero to jazz enthusiasts throughout Europe, particularly in the Soviet bloc, because of his nightly broadcasts in which he emphasized that freedom makes up the foundation of this art form. His commentary on the merits of improvisation stirred his vast audience.

Felix told me that the authorities kept on blocking the signal that brought his program to the Soviet Union. The Voice of America technicians knew this and would change the parameters of their signal every night. The Russian government did not want Soviet youth to hear this music, which they painted as propaganda about freedom in the Western world.

Felix and his friends would set up their short-wave radios and scan the ether until they picked up the program. The black market in Moscow was big business, and American jazz records brought the biggest big bucks, and in U.S. dollars.

Felix asked if I saw a lot of jazz in New York City. I told him that before I was married I lived just a few blocks from the Five Spot Café, where Thelonious Monk and John Coltrane recorded some of their mid-1950s hits. I shared that I was present during one of the recording sessions. His mouth dropped open when I told him that I had seen Charlie Parker and Billie Holiday at the 3 Deuces Jazz Club on 57th Street, that I was at Birdland at least once a week, and so on.

He couldn't believe that I had the freedom and the money to see the jazz greats that he worshiped. Each time he introduced me to his friends he would say: "This is my friend Ernie who is from New

York City and has actually seen Charlie Parker and Dizzy Gillespie and Art Tatum and Billie Holiday and John Coltrane and Art Blakey and George Shearing and Dave Brubeck!" It was like I had floated in from outer space and landed at the feet of a group of believers whose deity I had just visited.

Felix told me a wonderful story about what a group of his friends had done on May Day a few years earlier. In Moscow and maybe throughout the Soviet Union during the Cold War, there were groups of Russian youth called the Golden Boys. They were of college age and could be compared to American beatniks; they were West-oriented and very decidedly counterculture.

During those years, May 1 in the Soviet Union was a big holiday: the International Solidarity Day of Workers. As with all holidays, the Russian government took the opportunity to put on a show of its military power. Endless ranks of soldiers and sailors, tanks and armored vehicles, missiles, and military bands marched endlessly up the main thoroughfares of Moscow, passing the dignitaries on Red Square and continuing past the throngs of citizens who were encouraged to line the streets to honor their protectors.

On one particular May 1, Felix recounted, some of the Golden Boys decided to add a little spice to this boring event by introducing some up-tempo jazz to accompany the marching military. This was a very daring undertaking.

Here's the scene: Gorky Street passes in front of Red Square after turning onto it within a few hundred yards of the reviewing stand, which holds all of the waving Russian dignitaries. As the parade participants turn the corner, they straighten their lines, reposition their rifles, get in step, and attempt to look their best.

This was in the middle of Moscow's commercial district with mid-rise buildings lining the streets and snuggled up to the sidewalks. The ground floors contained stores, and the upper floors were offices, mostly for government use.

The intersection where the May Day parade makes a right turn from Gorky Street to go past the reviewing stand.

Felix told me that a group of his friends had been able to gain access to part of an upper floor in one of these buildings the night before the May 1 parade. They set up a radio with an alarm clock that would turn on a phonograph and lower the arm to the moving disc. Very large loudspeakers were placed at open windows and connected to the turntable. The activation time was set to the moment when the parade would be turning the corner and making its way in front of the reviewing stand.

Felix said the plan went flawlessly. The streets were filled with unenthusiastic flag-waving parade-goers. Then the alarm clock turned on the turntable, the record dropped, and the needle dropped on the disc. Out of the loudspeakers above the crowds, the military, the missiles, the tanks, and the marching bands came the very loud but oh-so-beautiful "St. Louis Blues March" played by the Glenn Miller Orchestra.

After a momentary freeze, Felix recalled, the crowds came to life and the flag waving met the decidedly blues beat of the recording. It lasted for a full three minutes before the location of the music was discovered and destroyed.

Felix never said that he was part of this undertaking, and he assured me that the producers of this event were never discovered.

As our typical American house was starting to take shape and the logistics were comfortable, Felix asked me if I would be interested in experiencing some authentic Russian food. He knew that what we were being fed at the hotel and what the on-site commissary had to offer fell far short of what he could offer. I reminded him that I could not travel outside a specific line in the Moscow area. He convinced me that, at the right time, this would not be a problem and that I would be safely returned to my hotel well within the curfew.

Felix met me at the hotel after I tucked in my crew with their cold beers. Within a few blocks, we walked through a densely populated, fairly rundown residential area. Old wooden two- and three-story buildings with marginal living units (I could see into one of them from my hotel room) lined the back streets in contrast to other residential areas that appeared newer and less dense.

We approached a building where a large crowd was milling around, mostly made up of young men, who were smoking heavily and coming and going from the street. The mood was jovial, and Felix was greeted with waves and nods. We walked into what appeared to be the basement of the building with a winding stone stairway that led to a smoke-filled room overflowing with people sitting around small tables. The large room had arched openings and concrete columns that reminded me of one of those romantic black-and-white Humphrey Bogart movies. But this scene was smoky and noisy with no piano, no romance, just people drinking vodka, smoking, and eating.

Russian cigarettes come in a variety of types based on price. The cheap ones, which were being smoked by most of the people I saw, were vile and lung-wrenching. The vodka was brought to the table in one-liter carafes, which is the maximum one person was allowed in a single sitting. The quality was pure alcohol with a hint of taste. After a couple of shots, however, quality never came into question.

Cheap cigarettes, with paper filters.

Fancy cigarette box cover.

Felix and I were here not for the cigarettes or vodka, however—we were here to eat. He guaranteed that I would experience a taste that could not be duplicated anywhere. We were going to feast on chicken Kiev, for which this basement restaurant was famous. The dish, originating in the Ukraine, is a cutlet of boneless chicken breast that has been softened by violent pounding and stuffed with a butter, garlic, and herb mixture, with an emphasis on the butter and garlic. It is then breaded and baked or deep-fried. Each chef has their own secret recipe for the stuffing and breading. Ours came steaming from the deep fryer, golden brown and crisp with an unrecognizable fresh green garnish.

I had a hard time believing that a deep-fried chicken cutlet could be considered a delicacy, but when I cut it with my fork, the hot aromatic butter nectar flooded my plate and pushed aside the smokiness of the atmosphere. As we mopped up our plates with fresh rye bread, I could see that Felix was happy he had brought me. He was sharing one of the few things that made his life tolerable.

Felix's life was blessed by his relationship with his girlfriend. He told me that because of the difficult living conditions and the density of their lives, it was difficult for them to find a place where they could be alone to spend some quiet, intimate time together. This usually happened in the park where our house was being built and close to Felix's present job as our logistics coordinator. I cannot remember her name, but I do recall that she was long and lean with Asian-European facial features that I do remember as breathtaking, especially compared to the chubby, dull, *babushka*-wearing women who lived in our designated zone. She was a student and also worked as a model in one of the fancy dress shops in the high-end district.

Every couple of days, Felix would appear on the job site with his girlfriend to bid us goodbye at the end of the workday. One day, as we were putting our tools away, I asked Felix where he and his girlfriend were coming from before they stopped at our site.

"From the bushes!" he responded unashamedly.

I must have blushed, as his girlfriend's reaction to my reaction was hysterical laughter.

PHOTOGRAPHS

I carried my camera everywhere; here are more of my favorites.
See more at www.erniehurwitz.com.

Interior of the Aeroflot plane.

Typical shopping area, probably on a Sunday with shops closed.

Soldier in foreground, as artists paint a street scene.

Painting in progress.

Russian bulldozer leveling the mud at the house site; materials container in the background. John is creating a door for our changing room/office.

Materials container transformed into All-State "Field Office" in Moscow.

George and Louis assembling roof trusses.

Roof truss assembly complete, set aside for later installation.

John and Odd on a sunny day discussing the next steps in house framing.

Odd prepares the plywood roof sheathing for the Russian carpenters.

Louie talking to Russian journalists about the model house construction site.

Air bladder lifting frame for a dome; there were a number of domes
at the exhibition.

Air bladder lifting frame for dome.

Dome frame with fully extended bladder, swimming pool in foreground.

Interior fabric hung on inside of bladder-lifted dome.

Split house design beginning to appear; note space for walkway where the
trusses are being stored.

John and Odd install exterior siding.

John watching Russian women laborers hauling mortar.

Truck entering split model home to dump asphalt for walkway.

Asphalt truck carefully inching into house walkway.

Asphalt truck exiting walkway through model home.

Early visitors touring the model home.

Russian visitors reading about the model home at the
American National Exhibition.

Exhibit of floor plan and explanation (in Russian) of ease of construction and purchasing
homes like this in America.

Exhibition kiosk showing design and layout of American suburban housing developments.

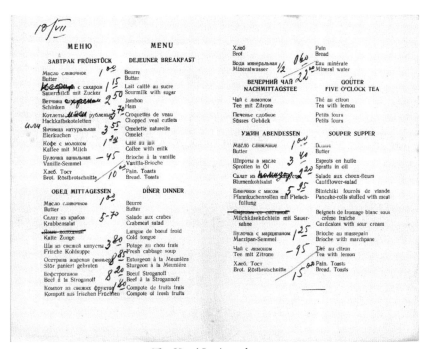

The Hotel Leningrad menu.

R. A. WATT COMPANY OF NEW JERSEY, INC.   P.O. Box 510   Freehold, New Jersey 07728   (201) 431-0566
A Subsidiary of Boise Cascade Corporation

February 7, 1969

Mr. William Safire
c/o Safire Public Relations, Inc.
375 Park Avenue
New York, New York

Dear Bill:

Congratulations on your recent appointment as Presidential
Assistant.

In a few months a decade will have passed since that famous
meeting in Moscow (I can remember vividly our traipsing through
downtown Moscow looking for the teletype office to get the story
out).

How about getting the cast of characters together and revisiting
the site?

Best personal regards,

aa

Ernest Hurwitz
Vice President

P.S. Whatever happened to that 35 mm. color shot I took of you,
Nixon and Krushchev coming from the Pepsi Cola exhibit to the
All-State house?

My letter to Billy in 1969.

THE WHITE HOUSE
WASHINGTON

February 21, 1969.

Mr. Ernest Hurwitz
Vice President
R. A. Watt Company of New Jersey, Inc.
P. O. Box 510
Freehold, New Jersey 07728

Dear Ernie:

Thanks for your note.

I hope you've done as well recounting
that Moscow experience as I have.

Best,

William Safire
Special Assistant
to the President

FEB 2 4 1969

A warm response from Billy.

7 BUILDING THE HOUSE

Louie using the shipping container transformed into a dressing room/field office.

Finally, about four days after we arrived, the first shipment of materials arrived by truck and was unloaded by Russian laborers while we checked the inventory. This shipment included all of the rough framing lumber that would make up the walls and ceilings. The wood roof trusses had been partially assembled in the United States, and we were to finish fabricating them on site. Everything we needed for this first phase was accounted for. We had almost a month to build this thing so we were relieved.

One of the early arriving shipping containers became our dressing room where we could change from street garb to work clothes. It was also a secure place to store our tools.

For the first few days we could not use our power tools because the electrical power setup in Russia is different from what we have in the United States. We needed a cycle converter to make things work, and that took a few days to procure. In the meantime, our crew was not happy using hand saws to cut the 2x4s.

Normally, after the house is rough-framed, the mechanical systems are installed in the walls and ceilings. The heating ducts, pipes for the plumbing, and electric lines are drilled through the 2x4 studs, and frames are made for the heating ducts. Since this house would not have a working plumbing or heating system, the furnace, sinks, and water closet would be dummied in. The only working mechanical would be the electrical system.

Russian electricians; the foreman is in the straw hat. Trained journeywomen were frequently part of professional crews.

The electrical work was done by a team of Russians, three men and two women. They were the first women I saw working on the exhibition; they weren't just laborers but were trained technicians. The team was led by a foreman and included a young apprentice who

perfect English. They came equipped with the cable that would
dergroud to the power source and shovels to dig the cable
       he ground. We supplied the cable that would be installed in the
house, together with all the necessary hardware.

Bonding with a Russian electrician.

The Russian team was very capable, and they did a lot of joking
around among themselves, mostly harmless male/female teasing and
showing off. Some of their time was spent in conversation with us
regarding the differences and the similarities of our lifestyles. We
were all young, in our 20s. Generally, the Russians were envious of
our freedom to choose to have fun or a family life but we were all
concerned about the political issues that separated us. These
conversations were kept to a minimum when their foreman was on
site.

Electricians burying the electric cable.

While the electricians buried the cable to bring electric service into the house, the carpenters John and Odd started laying out the 2x4 floor plates where the walls would rise. Louie and George, our drywall finishers and painters, started nailing the gusset plates that connected the partially-built roof trusses. These trusses were extra-long, as they needed to span not only the house but also the 10-foot walkway that split the house in half. Per our arrangement with the Russian government, we were provided with three skilled Russian carpenters to help us with the initial framing.

Exterior walls complete with roof trusses ready to be installed.

After the exterior walls were in place, we lifted the trusses and started the process of buttoning up the structure. It was important to make the structure watertight as quickly as possible so that we could work on the interior when it rained.

The process starts by attaching the plywood sheathing to the side walls and roof trusses. Driving nails through the plywood and into the 2x4s does not require much skill and can be time consuming and boring. Nailing machines did not exist at that time, and each nail had to be taken out of the pouch and hammered home. We decided to turn this part of the project over to our skilled Russian carpenters. Louie explained, in great detail, which nails were to be used and even demonstrated how the nail head should look after it was properly set. We tacked up a couple of the plywood sheets and struck a red chalk line indicating where to drive the nail so that it went directly into the truss. We drove a few nails indicating the spacing between them.

John prepares the plywood roof sheathing for Russian carpenters.

We were about a week into the project and the house was being enclosed with the plywood sheathing. The next step would be the installation of the roof shingles which would allow us to work on the interior in bad weather. The structure was starting to look like a house. I felt that this was a good opportunity to take the crew on a tour of the other construction sites, feeling secure that the plywood roof sheathing would be well on its way to completion when we returned.

Buckminster Fuller's futuristic geodesic dome was under construction in the exhibit and many advanced innovations were being used. At another site we watched an air bladder, which would increase in size, lift sections of steel pipe after attachments were made and more pipe added. There was no need for a crane or scaffolding. We were all very impressed with this technology.

After few hours we returned to our project to find our skilled Russian carpenters banging away on the roof of our house. Odd and Louie climbed up to inspect their work. From the ground it looked like there was a "situation." Odd was quite disturbed, and Louie was saying things to the Russians. I climbed the ladder to find out what the problem was. It seemed that the skilled Russian carpenters had used the red chalk line incorrectly. I saw that properly spaced nails were alternately driven on each side of the line rather than directly into the line as they had been instructed. This meant that the plywood was not attached to the wood trusses. Odd lifted a section of plywood in his rage to show the Russians how meaningless their work was. Louie told me that the Russians had misunderstood him and were sorry. None of us believed this and we were amazed that the Russians didn't slide off the roof with the unattached sheets.

U.S. crew chatting with Russian laborers.

By the time we were all on the ground, I asked Louie to thank the skilled Russian carpenters for their time and "not to come back tomorrow." The five of us climbed back to the roof and installed the plywood properly. Fortunately, we did not have to waste time pulling out the nails because they were just hanging there and we had plenty to spare.

The next day I was given a note to meet a U.S. embassy official. He told me that the Russians were part of my crew and that I could not fire them. I said that I appreciated their attempt to help, but I was on a tight schedule and this was not a training exercise. I told him that my crew was capable of completing the project on time. I did, however, request that one of the laborers remain, as he was an extraordinary worker and was very interested in what we were doing as well as being friendly and jovial.

I later found out that a few of the projects at the exhibition were either never completed or were only partially completed. In all these instances, Russian workers were involved. We had made the right choice.

Russian journalist takes a photo of Nikolai in front of the field office/dressing room.

The Russian laborer that we kept was named Nikolai. He was a steamfitter by trade but with our project he would do whatever he could to help. He made sure that the site was kept clean and that all of our material was in the right place and in order. He directed the unloading of the trucks and moved much of the material into its designated location. He stayed with the project after the house was completed and until the construction team returned to New York. The Macy's team continued to use Nikolai's services during the furniture-moving and decorating process.

Nikolai brings materials to the dump site.

One morning he didn't show up for work. I was concerned. By mid-morning, I was told that Nikolai had stolen something from our site and had been put in jail. I couldn't believe it, so I went to the Russian authorities to get the details. They acknowledged that he was in jail awaiting arraignment, even though I had not been notified about the theft. I asked what had been taken. They showed me the evidence. It was a piece of carpeting that was cut off from the roll and discarded. Nikolai found it in the disposal area and asked me if he could have it to take home. I said of course, not realizing that this was my mistake in not writing some kind of note saying that this had been given and not stolen. After explaining all of this to the jailers, it was agreed that he would be released but he would not be able to keep the carpeting. It would have to be trashed.

The next day I was called into the U.S. embassy for a conference. It seems that I had negotiated with the Russians for the release of Nikolai without notifying the embassy. I promised that I would not do it again.

After firing the skilled Russian carpenters and relying on the capabilities of my own men, we completed the house ahead of schedule. But there were some other minor situations where, if the Russians were involved, we would be wary.

One day a truck arrived with our plumbing fixtures and appliances. This is an exciting time, as the house was complete and we were adding the finishing touches. Nikolai supervised the unloading, which was being done by the Russian driver and his assistant. The bathroom sink, bathtub, and water closet were packed in protective boxes; damage would have been irreparable. I instructed Nikolai to tell the driver not to remove the items from the boxes, as we would do that when they were safely in the house. They just needed to be passed down to Nikolai who would bring them inside.

While he was taking the tub into the house, the driver, as if he had not heard the instructions, was removing the water closet from the box while it was still on the bed of the truck, unseen by us. Nikolai and I came out of the house and saw the blue American Standard toilet in the arms of the driver. As Nikolai rushed to the truck, the fixture was on its way to the ground and suddenly in pieces. Much loud Russian shouting was exchanged, and I had to get between Nikolai and the driver to cool things down. The driver vehemently apologized, saying he thought he was being helpful in removing it from the box but that it slipped when he went to put it down.

The possibility that something like this could happen was anticipated when the logistics were planned. Anything remotely breakable was packed and ready to be shipped from New York if the need arose. The telegram went out from the embassy; the new water closet was on the next plane and reached us with time to spare.

Macy's decorators were hanging pictures and installing *tchotchkes*, but the landscaping had not even started. The opening of the fair was just a few days away, and there were piles of dirt and mud all around the house. An extensive landscape plan had been developed that would tie all the exhibits together, but little of the work had been done or was even under way. Large trees had to be planted, and shrubs and flower beds installed. I was getting anxious.

Beginning of patio and walkway construction.

I went to the Russian engineer who was in charge of the entire operation and asked for an update. He assured me that everything was on schedule and not to worry. Even though at that time I would not consider myself a veteran in construction, I had already learned that the term "not to worry" actually meant "start to worry." There was nothing I could do except bother this engineer. His name was Abramoff, and he was a legend in the Russian construction trades. For example, some of the foundation work for the larger structures was installed in frozen ground, and Abramoff had come up with ways to ensure that the concrete cured before it froze. When I told him about our slab and its uncured look, he gave me a not-to-worry smile.

Russians installing brick patio, with Louie hanging around in case we needed a translator.

We had interesting discussions about some of the latest American construction projects under way in New York: the Guggenheim Museum's curved walls; the 59-story Pan Am building going up over Grand Central railroad tracks; and Robert Moses's Columbi Coliseum, where the Russians were exhibiting their product everyday life. Abramoff was fascinated and a bit sad that he was not doing that kind of innovative construction. He impressed me with his education. He had multiple engineering degrees, including electrical, civil, aeronautical, and mechanical. I had the feeling that he was frustrated by not being able to use his deep knowledge. As far as my landscaping was concerned, he continued to tell me not to worry and that everything would be beautiful.

Russian women laborers brought in for landscaping.

I waited patiently, and a couple of days before the pre-opening of the fair, a large bus and many dump trucks arrived at the site. The bus offloaded women who did not look like landscape workers: they were wearing kitchen aprons. They were handed shovels and rakes as they disembarked. The trucks contained dry earth and landscape material such as trees, shrubs, flowers, bedding, and fencing.

I asked Nikolai to check out what was happening, even though it was clear to me by that point that this was how work was sometimes accomplished in the Soviet Union. Nikolai had a conversation with one of the women, who told him that the bus had pulled up at the end of her street, blocking the intersection, and a truck did the same thing at the other end of the block. This prevented anyone from leaving the area. A loudspeaker announced that all residents had to get onto the trucks. I assumed that all the men were at work and that all the kids were in school, and I guessed that mothers with babies at home were exempt from this assignment. The remaining women became our landscape crew and I was "not to worry."

Landscaping crew transforming mud to lawn.

And then the magic happened. Within a short period of time, the aproned women's shoveling and raking and planting slowly transformed the mud into a pleasant suburban Long Island home site. The landscape supervision was directed by a couple of Russian men who worked with the New York-based landscape designer. The same bus arrived every morning, and the apron-wearing landscaping crew knew what needed to be done.

Suddenly, the house was finished. The punch lists were done. I began to visualize scores of people crowding down the walkway that split the house down the middle. There'd be pre-planned tours of special groups, schools, and military led by young Americans fluent in Russian. The furniture was in place and there was a 10-foot wide rubber welcome mat placed at the entrance. Louie had already left for home, and Odd, George, and John were as anxious to return home as I was to see them off. I needed time to stand back and survey what we had done without the responsibility of watching after my crew.

One of my only photos of the exterior of the finished house.

NOTE: I didn't take a photo of the finished kitchen because no one knew it was going to be famous. After the VIP reception, I left, not feeling the need to see U.S.-made products. And, I wanted to go on my postponed honeymoon.

Nikolai giving a tour to students, standing in front of the not-yet-famous kitchen.

Regular mail was handled through diplomatic pouches that went from the U.S. embassy in Helsinki to the embassy in Moscow. That's how I could send love letters to my bride and update my office back home on the house's progress. One day, after the house was completed, my crew had returned home and Macy's was in doing the decorating, I received a letter from Billy saying that there might be a problem getting the news out of Moscow after our house was visited by Khrushchev and Nixon. Russia had agreed to lift its news blackout policy during the time of the exhibition, but Billy didn't trust this. The telegrams I had sent were either from my hotel or from the embassy but he asked me to locate the central telegraph office in Moscow and find out the fastest way of getting there.

One of several telegrams I received from my boss during construction.

This was getting exciting. The telegraph office was on the second floor of a downtown office building accessible by a flight of stairs from the lobby. I walked up the stairs, entered through a glass door, and approached a person standing behind the counter. He spoke perfect English and, along with some small talk, responded warmly to my questions of how to send a telegram and the times the office was open.

Billy and my boss, Herb, would be arriving shortly, and I wanted to make sure that everything was ready for this vital visit of Khrushchev and Nixon, two of the world's most famous people. I had a couple of days of leisure time but spent most of it at the house checking and double-checking everything and visiting the other exhibits. Dozens of Russian-speaking American college students would be stationed around the house to guide the visitors and answer questions. I was later told that 4,500,000 visitors walked through the house, although this number is debatable.

We were informed that entrance to the exhibition would be controlled by tickets that were distributed to Communist Party card carriers, trust officials, and upper-management Russians who, in my opinion, might not be convinced that ours was a "typical American home." Indeed, this group might be skeptical of our claim that the American blue-collar worker could afford to buy this house. The average Russian person on the street might be more susceptible to the reality and were not generally welcomed to the fair. All of the exhibitors were given tickets to distribute to Russians who had participated in helping the exhibitors complete their projects.

Except for Nikolai, my team and the Macy's team ended up not using our assigned tickets which had been set aside for the Russian-assigned workers we had let go in the beginning of the project. At the end of the day, some of the Macy's people, the college students and I took the opportunity to distribute the extra tickets we had to people we saw strolling around the park. This went on for a couple of days until I was, once again, called into the U.S. Embassy for a meeting. It seems that what we were doing was angering the Russian establishment, and we were told to stop—immediately. We had wrongly assumed we were doing something very positive for American-Russian relations because all the people we gave tickets to were very happy and thanked us profusely.

Around this time, about two days before the opening, the newspaper and broadcast industry folks were arriving in Moscow to cover this anticipated newsworthy event. Before it was open to the Russian public, Nixon was to tour all of the exhibits to show Khrushchev and his entourage the American way of life.

A chartered plane with every famous American newsmen (yes, all men, it *was* 1959) and photographers arrived, and the atmosphere of the fairgrounds changed to the anticipation of some kind of world-class athletic event. What also changed was the usual crowd at the Amerikanski Dom. The bar hours were extended for the entire week. It was now a noisy, smoky bar, and not a private lounge where I could wind down.

George painting the model home yellow.

One morning I found myself sharing a cab with *The New York Times* Moscow bureau chief and a famous *Life Magazine* photographer. A new excitement prevailed.

This was going to happen, and I was in the middle of it.

8 SHOWTIME

Crowds in line to see the All-State Typical American Home.
From an All-State Properties press release, photographer unknown.

Billy arrived in Moscow with the rest of the press corp. He spent most of his time with his fellow agents, photographers, and other members of the press. When he and I toured the house, he showed me a schedule of the events that were planned for the grand opening. Nixon would be guiding Khrushchev through the exhibits and would spend five minutes in the typical American home.

Wow. This was super exciting for me—the vice president of the United States and the premier of the Soviet Union spending five minutes in a house that I built.

It was, of course, Billy's responsibility to ensure us, his client, that an adequate amount of notoriety would be given to this very expensive effort. Billy told me that Nixon pretty much guaranteed his appearance at the house in a letter he sent to Billy's boss, Tex McCrary. This is what I remember it said:

> *Tex,*
>
> *I certainly will stop at your client's Typical American Home when I'm in Moscow.*
>
> *My regards to Jinx.* [Jinx Falkenburg, actress, model, and McCrary's wife]
>
> *Dick*

I'm sure my boss saw this letter and was pleased with this promise.

I was in awe of the power that Billy's boss had and wondered how this kind of thing happens. I had known about Tex McCrary from a radio chat show that sounded like it came from the McCrary home on Long Island. Tex and Jinx would have a conversation over breakfast (there was always the sound of coffee cups in the background). Their talk was primarily about the current social situation in New York, including show business, Broadway, marriages, divorces, and rumors. On my drive to work, I would listen to them between the Bob & Ray and Klavan & Finch radio programs.

Final touches on model home before the opening.

On the day before the grand opening of the house, I did a final walk-through. The landscaping looked great, the beds were made, the pictures were level, the windows were clean, the directional signage was in the right place, and visitors would be able to read, in Russian, about some of the details of the typical American home.

I strolled through the expanded walkway that split the house in half and made sure that the wrought-iron railing, which was installed to keep people from entering the rooms, was secure. I put some pressure against the railing and pushed and pulled on it. When I got to the living room area, I pushed on one of the vertical posts embedded in the concrete. To my surprise it popped out, taking a large hunk of concrete with it and making the entire section of the railing quite wobbly.

Russian laborer spreads asphalt for walkway through model home
with railing in background.

I knew that we had installed the posts in uncured concrete, but luckily, this post seemed to be the only one that remained unsecured. Initially, we put metal sleeves into the drilled post holes. These sleeves were extra protection for the posts—I wanted to double the strength of the posts to withstand the stress that the railing would sustain with crowds of people leaning and pushing as they walked through the house. Little did I know that on the following day V.I.P.s would be leaning on the railing while the debate unfolded.

What if Nixon or one of the American or Soviet dignitaries leaned on the railing and the upright post popped out? Would I have shouted that it was the Russians who installed the concrete foundation? Would Nixon have made a sarcastic remark to Khrushchev about "Soviet superiority?" Would Khrushchev have lost it and taken off his shoe and banged it on the railing as he did in October of 1960 at the U.N., when a Security Council delegate said something he didn't like?

I was close to hysteria, but of course none of this actually happened.

Now I needed to get the railing fixed, but my crew had flown back home. I went over to a pavilion being built by a Texas construction company. The project manager and I had spent quality time at the Dom trading construction war stories and the comparative qualities of bourbon and scotch whiskies.

He had exactly what I was looking for: a bag of American-made ready-mix quick-set cement. With the help of one of the American students, we quickly reset the post with a high-grade product.

View of living room from walkway in completed house.

Early in the construction of American National Exhibition.

My boss arrived nervous and overwhelmed at the confusion of dignitaries and the press corps and the anticipation of the upcoming visit by Nik and Dick.

The next day, July 24, the opening ceremony started quietly. The weather was fine, a perfect summer's day. The typical American home was in perfect order. The newsmen and photographers were nursing their usual hangovers as they were corralled into a confined space in front of the platform where Nixon would give the opening address.

I had the proper credentials, so I pushed my way in with this group. While we waited for the ceremonies to begin, I overheard two photographers complaining that it would be impossible to get different shots of the proceedings because they were standing in the same space without the ability to move around. One of the photographers who always defied these restrictions was not in this group. *Life Magazine*'s Howard Sochurek usually pulled off photos at vantage points not accessible to his fellow newspeople. He was highly resented and respected for this. The game was finding him for this historic event.

He was not in one of the trees surrounding the speakers' platform, he was not in the back of a truck parked on the roadway, he was not in a helicopter or dangling from the end of a parachute.

"I found him!" someone shouted.

We turned to the shouter, who was pointing toward the roof of one of the pavilions. It was Sochurek. Everyone turned; cheers and fingers went up to salute him. Apparently, he had arrived a few days earlier and made an arrangement with one of the contractors to climb onto the roof for this event.

Nixon opened the exposition with boring ego-filled talk, and we followed him and Khrushchev as they toured the exhibit site.

The one-story main exhibition pavilion contained a vast cross-section of what made up American lives: clothing, shoes, toys, cigarettes, games, and books. Books about America. Books about free speech and freedom. Fiction and nonfiction stories of America's heroes and regular folks. I was told that in anticipation of the Russian visitors pocketing these written treasures, the supply was constantly restocked with English- and Russian-language books containing stories of abundance, democracy, and happy middle-class living. The Russians could read these books, as English was taught as a second language in Russian schools. This was a well-thought-out propaganda activity by the U.S. government.

Main exhibition building under construction, about three weeks before the opening.

I didn't want to get caught up in the crowd of photographers, newsman, translators, and dignitaries, so I lingered outside the pavilion waiting for Khrushchev and Nixon to exit and start moving toward the house. I was talking with one of the American students when he said, "Quick, turn around and get a picture."

Khrushchev was heading out the door behind me, ahead of his security and the parade that followed him. I turned around, raised my camera, and pushed the shutter. One of his security guards almost ran me over as he moved toward me. The guard tried to grab my camera but decided to stay with his boss, who was moving quickly in the opposite direction. Weeks later, after the photo was developed, it turned out to be an incredible close-up.

"Quick, turn around, it's Khrushchev!"

The group moved to the area of the fairgrounds where the RCA television studio had been set up. Next on the schedule was the Pepsi-Cola exhibit, then us. I felt like an actor standing in the wings, ready to go on stage, unable to remember any of my lines.

My boss was similarly anxious. The future of his company was just a few steps away.

Billy was attempting to steer the press into position so that they could take full advantage of our five minutes when the procession got to the house. But there was a delay at RCA, and the group did not follow the schedule for when they were to exit.

The cause of the delay was that Khrushchev started peppering Nixon with a whole bunch of issues while facing the camera and talking much faster than what the translator could convey to Nixon. When Nixon finally understood what was being said, he became livid, smiling but sweating. At that point the entourage exited the RCA studio and went to the Pepsi-Cola exhibit.

I had stationed myself between the house and the location of the entourage but returned to the house while they were sipping Pepsi.

After the group left the Pepsi-Cola exhibit, they didn't follow the prescribed walkway to the house. I saw that they were headed in the wrong direction and would either miss the designated entrance or encounter fences that had been installed to move people the correct way. By this time Billy came around the front of the group and started yelling at me and the student hosts, "Remove the fences!"

So we started pulling up the nicely-designed barriers, which were fortunately driven into the turf and not into concrete. Thanks to this confusion and the extra time spent in the RCA studio, there were now less than the five minutes allowed for the visit to the American house. The photographers and press who wanted to avoid getting trapped inside remained outside as Nixon and Khrushchev entered the wrong way.

The photographers were hovering outside the entrance when Nixon started to retaliate against Khrushchev. Our five minutes were up, but no one was moving. Nixon led Khrushchev to the kitchen and stopped. The translators, exhibition officials, and Soviet political hierarchy gathered around the two world leaders as Nixon started to unload on his stocky adversary. As Nixon relaxed into the debate, he actually put his foot on the railing. It was attached to the wall, not the concrete slab.

I thought about how fast I could get to the airport, but I decided to turn all of this energy and anxiety over to the Gods of Quickset cement so I could relax.

There was a bigger problem than a hastily-repaired post, however. History was in the making but the press was unable to record what was going on because both ends of the walkway were jammed with dignitaries and aides and the schedule called for a very short visit. And once the debate was happening the guards wouldn't let the press in. So Billy took control. He went over to a few of the photographers and told them that he would go into the kitchen where Nixon and Khrushchev were debating. If they could get their cameras to him, he would take the shots and they would get credit. I was at the entrance, so he told me to get the cameras and pass them over the heads of the people in attendance until they got to him in the kitchen.

The press and invited dignitaries unable to enter the house during the Kitchen Debate. Photographer unknown.

I remember holding Elliott Erwitt's Rolleiflex and thinking that this may have been the very camera that made him famous. We passed in many cameras, shouting to Billy the name of each photographer. One photo was of my boss, who was standing a few feet behind Khrushchev pointing at the camera and directing Billy where to take the shot. To this day it's unclear if Billy himself took the famous photo that appeared on the front page of the next day's *New York Times;* credit was given to Erwitt and various agencies.

The debate lasted for over 45 minutes. During this time, Billy was somehow able to arrange for Harrison Salisbury of *The New York Times* to climb over the railing and sit at the kitchen table to take down the commentary. This was a brilliant move. Billy knew that Salisbury didn't need translation, that he was proficient in the Russian language.

It was a scoop. My boss's demand and McCrary's Billy had pulled it off. Front page of *The New York Times*!

The Kitchen Debate was now a part of history. As the crowd moved out, Khrushchev stopped to indicate that he wanted to greet the builders of the house. I was summoned; I stood behind my boss and was introduced as the "foreman of construction." Nikita shook my hand. He applied a great deal of pressure and to this day I don't know if it was a friendly gesture or a reaction to Nixon's debating skills. Sadly, all the photographers were moving to the next exhibit, and I don't know if any photos were taken of Khrushchev and me.

We were all exhausted and shocked at the event. Billy and my boss disappeared, and I remained with the Macy's team recounting what had just happened. My boss returned a few minutes later with Billy to announce that he was able to obtain an invitation for us to dine with Nixon and the other exhibitors that evening at the Embassy.

There was something else going on. My boss seemed agitated and not in the joyous mood I would have expected after what had just happened. Billy said, "There's talk of a news blackout. I need to get to the telegraph office." Part of the negotiation for this exposition was that the Russian news blackout would be lifted. It was important to the sponsoring U.S. corporations to inform their stockholders of this global event.

I overheard, perhaps at the Dom, that the banter in the RCA studio and the Kitchen Debate had not gone well for Khrushchev, which may have fueled Russia's decision to reinstate the blackout. Billy wanted to try to head it off.

9 THE KITCHEN DEBATE

© Elliott Erwitt/Magnum Photos

As I reflected on what had just happened at our house—that Nikita Khrushchev and Richard Nixon had a global debate in *my* kitchen and that *The New York Times* had gotten an exclusive story—I just wanted to savor the moment.

Billy had a different idea.

"I need to get to the central telegraph office and get this story out before they drop the news blackout!" he said, interrupting my moment of reflection and pulling me out of the park to get a cab. Having heeded his previous instructions, I knew where we had to go and what we had to do to get there in a hurry. The cab driver did not need to be told to step on it, since fast is the only way the Russians drive.

We arrived at the telegraph office and Billy rushed out as I paid the cab driver. I ran up the stairway as he got to the top of the landing. When we approached the entrance door, I remember seeing a man inside the door locking it and putting up a sign that must have said "Closed."

Billy banged on the door holding a fistful of money. No response. I asked him what was going on. He said, "Something happened at the RCA studio that might reverse the Soviet's lifting the blackout ban. Let's get back to the park so I can get more information before tonight's dinner."

I don't know what happened at the television studio, but it must have pissed off the premier. One rumor was about recording what he said to Nixon and getting an assurance that it would be translated "word for word" for the American TV audience. Another rumor was that there had been an agreement not to record anything unless the Russians had an opportunity to review it.

The following is an excerpt of the recording that was captured on the Ampex color videotape at the RCA studio display (and which is available all over the internet these days):

Khrushchev: *[in jest]* You look angry, as if you want to fight me. Are you still angry?

Nixon: *[in jest]* That's right.

Khrushchev: ...and Nixon was once a lawyer? Now he's nervous.

Nixon: Oh, yes *[chuckling],* he still is [a lawyer].

Another Russian speaker: Tell us, please, what are your general impressions of the exhibit?

Khrushchev: It's clear to me that the construction workers didn't manage to finish their work and that the exhibit is still not put in order. This is what America is capable of, and how long has it existed? 300 years? 150 years of independence and this is her level? We haven't quite reached 42 years, and in another seven years we'll be at a level of America, and after that we'll go farther. As we pass you by, we'll wave "hi" to you, and then, if you want, we'll stop and say, "Please come along behind us." If you want to live under capitalism, go ahead, that's your question, an internal matter; it doesn't concern us. We feel sorry for you, but really, you wouldn't understand. We've already seen how you understand things.

Another U.S. speaker: Mr. Vice President, from what you have seen of our exhibition, how do you think it's going to impress the people of the Soviet Union?

Nixon: It's a very effective exhibit, and it's one that will cause a great deal of interest. I might say that this morning, very early this morning, I went down to visit a market, where the farmers from various outskirts of the city bring their items to sell. I can only say that there was a great deal of interest among these people, who were workers, farmers, etc. would imagine that the exhibition from that standpoint would, therefore, be a considerable success. As far as Mr. Khrushchev's comments just now, they are in the tradition we learn to expect from his speaking extemporaneously and, frankly, whenever he has an opportunity. I can only say that if this competition, which you have described so effectively, in which you plan to outstrip us, particularly in the production of consumer goods, if this competition is to do the best for both of our peoples and for people everywhere, there must be a free exchange of ideas. There are some instances where you may be ahead of us—for example in the development of the thrust of your rockets for the investigation of outer space. There may be some instances, for example, color television, where we're ahead of you. But in order for both of us to benefit…

Khrushchev: *[interrupting]* No, in the rockets we've passed you by, and in the technology…

Nixon: *[continuing to talk]* You see, you never concede anything.

Khrushchev: We always knew that the Americans were smart people. Stupid people could not have risen to the economic level that they reached. But as you know, "we don't beat flies with our nostrils!" In the 42 years we've made progress.

Nixon: You must not be afraid of ideas.

Khrushchev: We're saying it is you who must not be afraid of ideas. We're not afraid of anything.

Nixon: Well, then, let's have an exchange of them. We all agree on that, right?

Khrushchev: Good. *[Khrushchev turns to his translator and asks]* Now what did I agree on?

Nixon: *[interrupts]* Now, let's look at our pictures.

Khrushchev: Yes, I agree. But first I want to clarify what I'm agreeing on. Don't I have the right? I know that I'm dealing with a very good lawyer. Therefore, I want to be unwavering in my miner's girth, so our miners will say, "He's ours and he doesn't give in!"

Nixon: No question about that.

Khrushchev: You're a lawyer of capitalism, I'm a lawyer for Communism. Let's kiss.

Nixon: All I can say, from the way you talk and the way you dominate the conversation, is that you would make a good lawyer yourself. What I mean is this: Here you can see the type of tape which will transmit this very conversation immediately and this indicated the possibilities of increasing communication, and this communication will teach us some things and you some things too, because, after all you don't know everything.

Khrushchev: If I don't know everything, then you know nothing about Communism, except for fear! But now the dispute will be on an unequal basis. The apparatus is yours and you speak English while I speak Russian. Your words are taped and will be shown and heard; what I say about science won't be translated, and so your people won't hear it. These are not equal conditions.

Nixon: There isn't a day that goes by in the United States when we can't read about everything you say in the Soviet Union and, I can assure you, I never make a statement here that you don't think we can read in the United States

Khrushchev: If that's the way it is, I'm holding you to it. Give me your word. I want you, the vice president, to give me your word that my speech will be taped in English. Will it be?

Nixon: Certainly it will be. And by the same token, everything I say will be recorded and translated and will be carried all over the Soviet Union. That's a fair bargain.

[Both men shake hands and walk off, still talking.]

By this time Nixon needed some ammunition to counter Khrushchev's claim of the superiority of his "young" nation. And our house was a perfect spot for Nixon to retaliate. When they walked into the house, Nixon headed for the kitchen… and so started what became known as the Kitchen Debate.

Contact sheet © Elliott Erwitt/Magnum Photos. You can see Safire in the kitchen and Harrison Salisbury sitting at the kitchen table getting an exclusive for *The New York Times*.

Nixon: I want to show you this kitchen. It is like those at our houses in California *[Nixon points to the dishwasher]*.

Khrushchev: We have such things.

Nixon: This is our newest model. This is the kind which is built in thousands of units for direct installations in the houses. In America, we like to make things easier for women.

Khrushchev: Your capitalistic attitude toward women does not occur under Communism.

Nixon: I think that this attitude toward women is universal. What we want to do is to make life easier for our housewives. This house can be bought for $14,000, and most Americans [veterans from WWII] can buy a home in the bracket of $10,000 to $15,000. Let me give you an example that you can appreciate. Our steel workers, as you know, are on strike. But any steel worker could buy this house. They earn $3.00 an hour. This house costs about $100 a month to buy on a contract running 25 to 30 years.

Khrushchev: We have steel workers and peasants who can afford to spend $14,000 for a house. Your American houses are built to last only 20 years. So builders can sell new houses at the end. We build firmly. We build for children and grandchildren.

Nixon: American houses last more than 20 years, but, even so, after 20 years, many Americans want a new home or a new kitchen. Their kitchen is obsolete by that time. The American system is designed to take advantage of new inventions and new techniques.

Khrushchev: This theory doesn't hold water. Some things never go out of date—houses, for instance. Furniture, furnishings perhaps, but not houses. I have read much about America and American houses, and I do not think that this exhibit and what you are saying is strictly accurate.

Nixon: Well, um…

Khrushchev: I hope I have not insulted you.

Nixon: I have been insulted by experts. Everything we say [on the other hand] is in good humor. Always speak frankly.

Khrushchev: The Americans have created their own image of the Soviet man. But he is not as you think. You think the Russian people will be dumbfounded to see these things, but the fact is that newly built Russian houses have all this equipment right now.

Nixon: Yes, but…

Khrushchev: In Russia, all you have to do to get a house is to be born in the Soviet Union. You are entitled to housing. In America, if you have a dollar, you have the right to choose between sleeping in a house or on the pavement. Yet you say we are the slaves to Communism.

Nixon: I appreciate that you are very articulate and energetic…

Khrushchev: Energetic is not the same as wise.

Nixon: If you were in the Senate, we would call you a filibusterer! You *[Khrushchev interrupts]* do all the talking and don't let anyone else talk. This exhibit was not designed to astound you but to interest you. Diversity, the right to choose, the fact that we have 1,000 builders building 1,000 different houses is the most important thing. We don't have one decision made at the top by one government official. This is the difference.

Khrushchev: On politics, we will never agree with you. For instance, Mikoyan likes very peppery soup. I do not. But this does not mean that we don't get along.

Nixon: You can learn from us, and we can learn from you. There must be a free exchange. Let the people choose the kind of house, the kind of soup, the kind of ideas they want.

During this back and forth, as they stood at the kitchen, the conversation heated up. This is where the finger-pointing Nixon moved the discussion in another direction with the red-faced Khrushchev.

Nixon: Would it not be better to compete in the relative merit of washing machines than in the strength of rockets?

Khrushchev: Yes, but your generals say we must compete in rockets. We are strong and we can beat you.

Nixon: In this day and age to argue who is stronger completely misses the point. With modern weapons it just does not make sense. If war comes, we both lose. *[Khrushchev starts to interrupt.]* I hope that the prime minister understands all the implications of what I just said. Whether you place either one of the powerful nations in a position so that they have no choice but to accept dictation or fight, then you are playing with the most destructive power in the world. When we sit down at a conference table it cannot be all one way. One side cannot put an ultimatum to another.

Khrushchev: Our country has never been guided by ultimatums. It sounds like a threat.

Nixon: Who is threatening?

Khrushchev: You want to threaten us indirectly. We have powerful weapons, too, and ours are better than yours if you want to compete.

Nixon: Immaterial. I don't think that peace is helped by reiterating that you have more strength than us, because that is a threat too.

This went on and on. Nixon pretty much out-talked Khrushchev for the rest of the hour in our kitchen. Harrison Salisbury captured the moment in a story that appeared on the front page of *The New York Times* on July 25, the day after the debate.

Nothing like the Nixon-Khrushchev exchange had ever occurred right in front of the press. Salisbury sat at the feet of the vice president and the premier, taking down each word.

Even to correspondents familiar with Khrushchev's capacity for catch-as-catch-can conversation and Nixon's ability to field rhetorical line drives, the day seemed more like an event dreamed up by a Hollywood script writer than a confrontation of two of the world's leading statesmen.

By the end of the debate, my energy had drained away. I had accomplished what I was asked to do. And the results were more than what was expected. I had a sense of satisfaction, but I was anxious to be with my bride, eat food that actually tasted like it came from a plant or animal, and live where drab was not the basic background color.

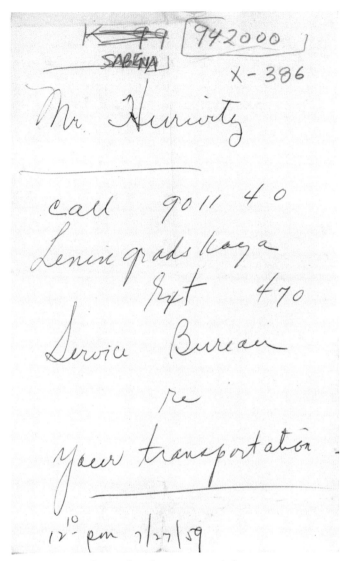

Preparations for my return trip home.

I don't know if the press blackout ever happened. The photo that Billy may have taken was wired to *The New York Times* so that it hit the front page with Salisbury's commentary. Since Billy never mentioned this, my guess is that Salisbury had methods for getting the story out.

10 DINNER AND DRAMA

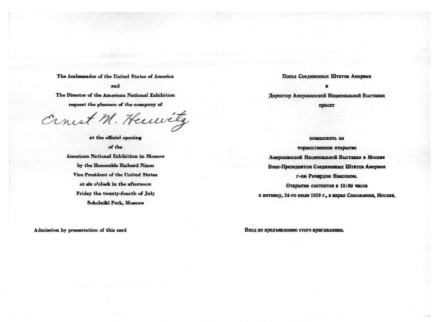

Invitation from the Honorable Richard Nixon.

After the debate, the American embassy put on a banquet for about a hundred people who had participated in the exhibition, including members of the press, exhibitors, designers, and contractors.

My boss, Billy, and I were ushered into a large hall that reminded me of the ornate venues that host weddings or bar-mitzvah receptions. People were milling around with drinks and typical American snacky things.

"We're in Russia, for God's sake," I said. "How about some caviar and blinis?" Actually, the little wrapped hot dogs and miniature pizza slices were a welcome change from the beigeness of the Russian cuisine.

We sat down at a round table and the speeches started. Exhibition officials, embassy officials, and finally Vice President Nixon spoke to the group. Nixon boasted about his domination over Khrushchev in our typical American home. He went on and on, with an increasing expansion of his ego as he sipped away at his drink. His constant sipping began to cause a slurring of his speech and a slight sway to his posture.

As we left after dinner, we were invited to meet the vice president in a reception line at the embassy's front entrance. The photographers took their place at the bottom of the stairs as the reception line passed Nixon, who provided handshakes and nods.

As I approached Nixon, he drew me out of the line so that we faced the cameras. He said something like, "I'm so glad that you could be here." He had his arm around my shoulder, not speaking to me but to the cameras.

I slithered away and continued walking down the stairs. Billy and my boss were meeting with officials, so I found a cab and told the driver *"Amerakanski Dom, pozhaluysta!"*

The Dom was jammed, mostly with the press corps excitedly discussing the events of the day, especially the Kitchen Debate. One of the reporters, or perhaps he was a photographer, was asking people at the bar if they were on the next day's morning flight to Brussels and on to New York. He was not asking members of the press, just people like myself and others who were involved with the exhibition. He had a metal canister in his hand and was asking if someone would deliver it to New York City.

I asked what this was all about and got this story: At the color television exhibit in the RCA pavilion, the Soviets had directed the exhibitor to make sure that no film was placed in the camera. The news blackout had been lifted and, as I was told, the Russians were concerned that Khrushchev might say something that could affect the temporary *détente* that this fair had been designed to achieve. Color tape was used for the purpose of showing Khrushchev the technological achievement of color television. I believe it was actually played back to him during the time in the studio, but I don't know if this was the same tape that was in the container that needed to be on the next flight out of Russia.

Since I was not leaving Moscow for a couple of days, I didn't offer to carry the canister. I wanted to see how the house held up when the fair opened. The first few days after the opening were restricted to a limited number of Russian VIPs. I was not around when the general public was admitted, and I never did get an accurate number of how many people passed through the house.

Visitors streaming out after viewing model home. Photographer unknown.

The bar at the Dom was a place where all the whispering, rumors, and facts were being discussed. This is what I heard, the next day, about the RCA film. The canister somehow made it to New York. After getting off the plane, the messenger was to give it to a designated person who would rush it to NBC and put it on the air with the announcement: "Interrupting this program with a news bulletin."

But it didn't happen.

What I was told did happen was that the messenger got off the plane and before he went through customs, he was met by official government people who identified themselves and asked for the canister containing the tape.

The rumor was that these people were Russians attached to the Soviet embassy in New York and that they obtained the canister in purportedly international territory.

Another rumor was that the film was picked up by our own Federal authorities who made sure that the content, which clearly showed Khrushchev's dominance over Nixon, would not be shown. It was in the kitchen that Nixon was able to turn the debate into a more neutral status before he hammered Khrushchev.

That was it. No blackout. No NBC exclusive. No embarrassing moments for two men who had access to the red button.

Adding my own theory to the possibilities, thinking of Nixon's Watergate reputation and his attempts to alter history, the canister pickup could have been orchestrated by the man himself. Having tape in the camera could have been on his menu to be used if that part of the debate was in his favor. Khrushchev had his own good reasons for the film not to be broadcast.

Or maybe it was a major U.S. news corporation breaking the rules to get an exclusive story.

The official word is that the tape was reviewed by Russian and American authorities and released for public view.

11 DASVIDANYA (GOODBYE)

A treasured postcard from Felix, 1960.

It was time to leave Moscow and reintroduce myself to my bride. When I told Felix I was leaving, he wanted us to get together in the park so that we could say goodbye. He brought his girlfriend, and we had tea at the fair's commissary. We promised we would write to each other. He didn't know what the future would bring, so he lived day by day with a casual attitude that hid a dark underside. We hugged, and his girlfriend took a ring off her finger and asked me to give it to my wife. We were all in tears.

Inside the GUM department store.

As I left Sokolniki Park for the last time, I thought that Felix and his girlfriend and I, in another setting, would have been close friends. And I knew I would never see them again.

I returned to the GUM department store to pick up the gifts for my family and friends. There was probably a better selection in the District, but I intended to keep up my boycott of that part of town.

That meant that I would not fulfill the promise to my mother to bring her a fur hat. I knew she would understand when I told her the story of my discovery of the economic divide of the Russian community. I had the feeling that this kind of disappointment was familiar to her when she lived in Bolshevik Lithuania a few decades earlier.

I found beautifully hand-crafted and exquisitely lacquered jewelry boxes and briarwood cigarette boxes to bring home. I was also able to obtain a couple of bottles of that great Russian champagne that we had too much of at the extravagant Hotel Ukraina dining room.

The next morning I was off on a direct flight to Paris with the excitement of being with my wife for a couple of weeks touring France, having good food, discovering Rhone Valley wine, and being open and a bit apprehensive about what adventure would come next. Like Felix, I had no idea what the future might bring, but at least I would be living in a country where there was considerably more room for optimism.

EPILOGUE

Luggage tag.

Honeymooning in Paris and Southern France kept me away from the news of the day and the very positive results of the Kitchen Debate.

I returned to work and concentrated on the Long Island projects with an occasional visit to the first out-of-state All-State Properties projects: a 400-house single family development just outside of Louisville, Kentucky.

I was being primed as the project manager. The Kentucky project was already under construction and had a small staff that I was to lead. At the time I thought this was a promotion for the success of the Russia gig even though it was never presented that way.

Shelter became my passion. The privilege of building houses was how I could create a personal legacy. Even though the bulldozers were removing trees and changing the surface of the earth, I considered what I was doing was similar to that of farming. Families would sleep, eat, play, and grow in my houses which then became their homes.

ABOUT THE AUTHOR

Ernie at the Moscow construction site with his ever-present camera hanging around his neck, a box of Kent cigarettes in his pocket, and the 1950s version of a hard hat: the Dobbs straw fedora.

Ernie Hurwitz was born on Mother's Day, 1932 in Rochester, New York. His family moved to New York City in 1949 where he completed high school and began his career as a homebuilder.

New York University night school was financed by Ernie's first mentor, who owned a large mortgage banking firm representing the largest Long Island and Manhattan real estate developers (Levitt and Sons of Levittown fame was his prime client).

Ernie lived on St. Mark's Place on the Lower East Side during this time and spent as much time as possible with the two loves of his life: the always-dancing, Modigliani-esque Ruth, who became his wife, and the jazz music of the 1950s.

Not wanting mortgage banking as a career, Ernie became employed by a large Long Island housing developer and mentor who put him into the trenches of the housing business. This company got him to Russia and his 15 minutes of fame.

He project-managed the construction of over 6,000 housing units for major developers in Kentucky, Washington, D.C., the Detroit area and New Jersey, including Levitt and Sons.

Anna, Martha, Dan, and Lila were born along the way.

Returning to New Jersey, he managed real estate in New York City and built custom homes near the Delaware Water Gap with an old friend and partner.

Retreating from the corporate and partnership world, Ernie formed his own construction management firm and acted as an owner's representative for developers and attorneys, and worked as an Arbitrator for the American Arbitration Association.

His projects were as diverse as mansion renovation, high rise consultation, urban redevelopment, and scores of kitchen, bath and apartment renovations.

Ernie and Ruth (now Kaveri) moved from Brooklyn to Seattle in 2012 to be close to 75% of their children and their two grandchildren.

They return every summer to their beloved "farm" in the Catskill Mountains to be off the grid in the small 1860s farmhouse they have owned since 1979.

Ernie continues to offer his pro bono construction management experience to a nonprofit foundation with historic buildings in New York City and Boston and campuses in Oakland and New York State.

"I am a storyteller… not a writer," is one of Ernie's mantras.

He also claims to be a leading expert on the art of parallel parking and the music of Thelonious Monk.

Moscow, 1959.

New York, 2019.

Made in the USA
Middletown, DE
04 January 2021